Questions in Hotel Reception

Questions in Hotel Reception

JEAN BULL, LHCIMA, CertEd(FE)
Lecturer in Food Service, North Star College, Swindon

and

GORDON BULL, MHCIMA, CertEd(FE)
Lecturer in Reception Studies, Salisbury College of Technology

STANLEY THORNES (PUBLISHERS) LTD

First published in 1981 by Stanley Thornes (Publishers) Ltd,
Educa House, Old Station Drive, off Leckhampton Road,
Cheltenham, Glos. GL53 0DN.

British Library Cataloguing in Publication Data

Bull, Jean
Questions in hotel reception.
1. Receptionists
2. Hotels, taverns, etc — Great Britain — Employees
I. Title   II. Bull, Gordon
647′.6   TX911.3.R/

ISBN 0 85950 310 0

Text typeset by TECH-SET, Unit 3, Brewery Lane, Nest Road, Felling, Tyne & Wear.
Printed and bound in Great Britain by Ebenezer Baylis & Son Ltd, Worcester and London.

Contents

INTRODUCTION		vii
PART ONE	**HOTEL ORGANISATION** Hotel departments: kitchen, restaurant, housekeeping. Structure, duties and relationship with reception	1
PART TWO	**THE HOTEL RECEPTIONIST** Personal attributes, social skills, modes of address, selling, marketing, fire and First Aid	10
PART THREE	**ADVANCE RESERVATIONS** Methods, procedures and law	14
PART FOUR	**RECEPTION PROCEDURES** Registration, computers and law	20
PART FIVE	**CASHIERS** VAT, service charge, methods of payment, foreign exchange	28
PART SIX	**BOOK KEEPING** Tabular ledger theory, machine accounting theory and computers	37
ANSWERS		
	HOTEL ORGANISATION	44
	THE HOTEL RECEPTIONIST	53
	ADVANCE RESERVATIONS	56
	RECEPTION PROCEDURES	62
	CASHIERS	67
	BOOK KEEPING	71
BIBLIOGRAPHY		85

Introduction

This book aims to provide a selection of questions under various topics concerned with hotel reception duties as covered in the following courses: City and Guilds 705 and 709, OND, HND, TEC diploma and certificate and also the BEC General Office Studies.

The book is for both lecturers and students alike and can be used as a revision aid at the end of each topic as well as at the end of the course when preparing for final examinations. It includes multiple-choice questions (worth 1 mark), short-answer questions (worth 5 marks) and longer-answer questions (worth 20 marks).

Multiple-choice questions are the most widely applicable and useful type of objective test item. They can measure simple learning outcomes as well as more complex outcomes concerned with knowledge, understanding and application. Each question consists of a direct question or incomplete statement called a *stem* and four suggested solutions called *alternatives*. One of these is the correct answer and the rest are called *distractors*.

For example:

Which city is the capital of America? (*stem*)

a New York	(*distractor*)	
b Washington	(*correct answer*)	*alternatives*
c Chicago	(*distractor*)	
d Boston	(*distractor*)	

The student must read the question carefully and choose the correct answer. He may then either mark his choice on an answer sheet or circle the letter of his choice in the book. No more than 100 questions should be attempted at one sitting. (The City and Guilds 709 examination offers 50 questions in one hour.)

Some questions simply involve choosing the correct answer. In other questions where application of knowledge is being tested, the *best* answer may have to be chosen. This will show whether or not the student understands the problem.

For example:

What is the most important purpose of the family car?

ⓐ mobility

b status symbol

c economy

d occasional outings

Other questions involve matching words and phrases given in two lists. A matrix is provided giving possible alternatives and the student must again choose the alternative which gives the correct solution.

For example:

Match the countries in List I with their capital cities in List II.

List I		List II	
A	Spain	1	Canberra
B	Australia	2	Bonn
C	Norway	3	Madrid
D	Germany	4	Oslo

a

A	B	C	D
1	2	3	4

b

A	B	C	D
1	4	3	2

c

A	B	C	D
1	3	4	2

ⓓ

A	B	C	D
3	1	4	2

A simpler variation is also given where the student must choose the alternative in which the correct order of a specific procedure is described.

For example:

Which of the following describes the correct procedure for making a pot of tea?

1 Pour on boiling water

2 Brew for 5 minutes

3 Heat the water and warm the pot

4 Add tea leaves to the pot.

a 1, 2, 3 and 4

b 3, 4, 2 and 1

c 2, 3, 4 and 1

ⓓ 3, 4, 1 and 2

A type of multiple-choice question which is especially useful for the revision of a particular topic is shown below. The question below consists of five lettered headings followed by a list of numbered questions. For each numbered question select the one heading which is most closely related to it. Each heading may be used once, more than once, or not at all.

a St. Louis
b San Francisco
c Chicago
d Los Angeles

1 Which city is in Southern California? (answer **d**)
2 Which city is on the Great Lakes? (answer **c**)
3 Which city is on the Mississippi? (answer **a**)
4 Which city is in Missouri? (answer **a**)

The student must choose, from the information given, the answers to the questions. This means that the subject matter can be tested from various angles.

Long-answer or essay-type questions should have a planned structure. A clear introduction setting the framework of the answer, the answer itself, and a reasoned conclusion summarising the main points. Answers may also be illustrated with the student's own experiences in the catering industry.

We hope that this book will fill the gap between the tests found in most textbooks and the multiple-choice tests now widely used on examination papers and give students opportunity to practise answering these types of questions. However, the questions in this book are only a selection of those the student might be expected to answer in an examination and are intended for practice. Success in these questions, therefore, cannot guarantee success in the examination, but the book will be a useful revision aid.

It must also be remembered that in spite of movement towards standardisation in the hotel reception, individual practices may vary. For example, hotels may use 'X' or '+' to indicate a double-bedded room on a reservation chart. However, all the examples used in the text are drawn from common practice.

Jean and Gordon Bull
June 1981

Part One
Hotel Organisation

Multiple-choice Questions (1 mark each)

1 Match the positions in List I with the appropriate description in List II.

List I		List II	
A	chef de rang	1	carver
B	maître d'hôtel	2	station waiter
C	maître d'hôtel de carré	3	wine waiter
D	sommelier	4	head waiter
E	trancheur	5	station head waiter

a

A	B	C	D	E
5	2	4	1	3

b

A	B	C	D	E
2	4	3	1	5

c

A	B	C	D	E
2	4	5	3	1

d

A	B	C	D	E
4	5	2	3	1

2 Where does the chef d'étage serve food and drinks?

a guest's room
b lounge
c coffee shop
d poolside

3 The legislation which states that menu prices must be displayed outside a restaurant is the:

a Labelling of Food (Amendment) Regulation 1972.
b Tourism (Sleeping Accommodation Price Display) Order 1977
c Price Marking (Food and Drink on Premises) Order 1979
d Price Marking (Drinks on Premises) Order 1975.

4 Match the copy of the waiter's triplicate check in List I with its appropriate destination in List II.

List I
A top copy
B bottom copy
C flimsy copy

List II
1 cashier
2 waiter's sideboard
3 kitchen

a

A	B	C
1	3	2

b

A	B	C
3	1	2

c

A	B	C
2	1	3

d

A	B	C
3	2	1

5 Match the types of menu in List I with the appropriate description in List II.

List I
A carte du jour
B table d'hôte
C à la carte
D plat du jour

List II
1 special dish of the day
2 dishes individually priced and cooked to order
3 special menu of the day
4 set meal at a set price

a

A	B	C	D
3	4	2	1

b

A	B	C	D
1	2	4	3

c

A	B	C	D
4	3	2	1

d

A	B	C	D
2	1	3	4

6 Which of the following gives the correct sequence of courses on a classical French menu?

a farineuses, hors d'oeuvre, entremets, poisson, entrée
b entrée, entremets, poisson, hors d'oeuvre, farineuses
c hors d'oeuvre, farineuses, poisson, entrée, entremets
d hors d'oeuvre, poisson, entrée, entremets, farineuses.

7 Which fruit juice can be served with Worcestershire sauce?

a orange
b grapefruit
c pineapple
d tomato.

8 If a guest phoned down to reception and asked for a bottle of 'Perrier' to be sent up, what would they require a bottle of?

a wine
b mineral water
c fruit juice
d aperitif.

The questions below consist of a list of four lettered countries followed by a list of numbered wines. State which country each comes from by choosing the appropriate letter. Each letter may be used once, more than once or not at all.

a Italy b Germany c France d Spain

9 Moselle

10 Sauternes

11 Chianti

12 Soave

13 Which area of France produces claret wine?

a Loire
b Côtes du Rhône
c Bordeaux
d Burgundy

The questions below consist of four lettered predominant flavours of liqueurs, followed by a list of brands of liqueur. For each numbered question, select the flavour which is most closely related to it. Each flavour may be used once, more than once or not at all.

a orange b mint c coffee d cherry

14 Kahlua

15 Grand Marnier

16 Crème de Menthe

17 Cointreau

18 Curaçao

19 Marachino

20 Tia Maria

21 If a guest asked for the sweetest sherry that you had available, which of the following would you offer?

a fino
b oloroso
c amontillado
d manzanilla

22 Match the wedding anniversaries in List I with their appropriate name in List II.

List I		List II	
A	25 years	1	ruby
B	40 years	2	golden
C	50 years	3	diamond
D	60 years	4	silver

a

A	B	C	D
4	1	3	2

b

A	B	C	D
3	4	2	1

c

A	B	C	D
3	4	1	2

d

A	B	C	D
4	1	2	3

23 Place the following people in the correct order in which they should stand to greet the guests at a wedding reception.

1 matron of honour
2 bridegroom's father
3 bride's mother
4 best man
5 bride
6 bride's father
7 bridegroom
8 bridegroom's mother

a 8, 2, 3, 6, 4, 1, 5, 7
b 3, 6, 8, 2, 5, 7, 4, 1
c 6, 3, 2, 8, 7, 5, 1, 4
d 5, 7, 4, 1, 3, 6, 8, 2.

Below is a list of kitchen staff. Indicate by their letter the approriate answer to the following questions. Each may be used once, more than once, or not at all.

a sous chef b chef garde manger c chef de cuisine
d chef tournant

24 Who is in charge of the whole kitchen?

25 Who is the assistant head chef?

26 Who is the relief chef?

27 What activity takes place in the stillroom?

a preparation of beverages, toast and bread and butter
b washing up
c service of meals from the kitchen
d dispensing of alcoholic beverages for the restaurant.

28 Due to the late departure of a guest, you have been asked to clean a bedroom with private bathroom. Place the following in the correct order to tackle the job.

1 dusting and polishing furniture
2 changing the bed
3 vacuuming the carpet
4 cleaning the bathroom.

a 3, 1, 2, 4
b 2, 3, 1, 4
c 1, 2, 4, 3
d 2, 1, 4, 3.

29 How much time is allowed for 'drinking up' in the bar of an on-licensed establishment?

a 5 minutes
b 10 minutes
c 15 minutes
d 20 minutes.

30 If liquor is supplied with a meal in a restaurant, how much time is allowed for 'drinking up' after permitted hours?

a 10 minutes
b 20 minutes
c 30 minutes
d 40 minutes.

31 Which of the following licences must be applied for to extend the hours of a fully licensed establishment for an afternoon wedding reception?

a special order of extension
b special hours certificate
c occasional licence
d special order of exemption.

32 Under the Weights and Measures Act 1963, which alcoholic beverages require a notice to be displayed indicating the measure by which they are sold?

a whisky, gin, rum vodka
b brandy, gin, rum, vodka
c gin, whisky, port, brandy
d rum, vodka, whisky, brandy.

33 At what age may a person drink beer with a substantial meal in a restaurant?

a 15
b 16
c 17
d 18.

Short-answer Questions (5 marks each)

34 Describe five of the following terms used in connection with food and beverage service:

(*a*) corkage
(*b*) mise en place
(*c*) gueridon
(*d*) dumb waiter
(*e*) aboyeur
(*f*) demi-tasse.

35 Draw and label the correct place setting for a table d'hôte menu.

36 Illustrate with a labelled diagram, how you would lay a tray for early morning tea for one.

37 Explain what would be served for:

(*a*) a full English breakfast
(*b*) a Continental breakfast.

38 Name the following glasses and suggest a drink that might be served in each.

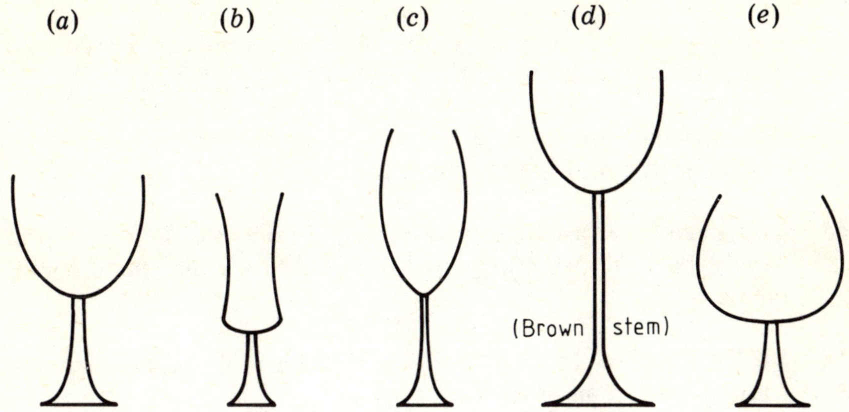

39 Study this French table d'hôte and make any corrections necessary. (There is one mistake in each dish.)

Jus à tomate
Oeuf mayonaise
Consomme royale

★ ★ ★

Fillet de plie meunière

★ ★ ★

Poulet sautée chasseur
Côte de boeuf rôti, sauce raifort

Pommes rôti
Pommes duchess
Bruxelles choux
Carrotes au beurre

★ ★ ★

Bavorois au chocolate
Crêpes au citröen
Glace à la vanille

★ ★ ★

Cafe

40 Draw a page to be duplicated to form a comprehensive hotel restaurant bookings diary. Enter three bookings to show how it would work.

41 List five of the chefs de partie in a large traditional hotel kitchen, and indicate the dishes which are prepared by each.

42 What is the purpose of a bin card in stores control? Illustrate your answer with a drawing of a bin card.

43 You have been asked to give your opinion as to how lost property should be dealt with in your hotel. Outline your recommendations below.

44 Briefly describe five of the following terms in relation to the uniformed staff of an hotel:

(*a*) société des Clefs d'Or
(*b*) linkman
(*c*) valet
(*d*) lodge
(*e*) luggage pass
(*f*) watchman's time clock.

45 Explain each of the following terms in relation to the housekeeping department of an hotel:

(*a*) bedboard
(*b*) occupancy list
(*c*) linen room
(*d*) OOO
(*e*) studio bedroom.

Long-answer Questions (20 marks each)

46 Design a comprehensive banqueting memorandum to be used by front office staff for guests wishing to book a function.

47 Design a comprehensive conference/exhibition booking form to be used by front office staff for organisers wishing to book a function.

48 A guest arrives early and you see that their room is not ready. On contacting the housekeeper, she informs you that the room has been cleaned, but not checked. As she is busy, she asks you to check the room before allowing the guest in. List the points you would look for in a completed room.

49

Across

1 All inns must provide food, drink and — (13)
7 Residents in an hotel expect this to be good (7)
8 This is issued when a guest pays cash (7)
9 A dog in the kitchen? (4,7)
14 Food items that may come from Brazil (4)
15 The hotelier should always — to please (3)
16 Deposit (10)
18 A type of lettuce (3)
19 A bottle for champagne (6)
20 One of your joints — but you don't cook it! (5)
21 Credit card (6)

Down

1 Full board (8,4)
2 Head porters (10)
3 A car or short skirt? (4)
4 Commissionaires may greet guests when they — (6)
5 A tall purple flower with a girl's name (4)
6 Requirement (4)
7 Seat at the bar? (5)
10 A man who likes good beer may ask for this (1,4,3)
11 A single item of furniture (4)
12 An odd spirit? (3)
13 Helped (8)
15 Beastly source of food (6)
17 They are read at the table (5)
18 A fuel or what you drink with 12 down (4)

50 (*a*) Briefly describe the benefits of interdepartmental co-operation within the hotel.

(*b*) Give examples of situations where co-operation is important between the front office and each of the other hotel departments.

Part Two

The Hotel Receptionist

Multiple-choice Questions (1 mark each)

Below are four modes of address. Select the correct one to use when first speaking to the following people. Each letter may be used once, more than once or not at all. Indicate your answer by using the appropriate letter.

a Your Royal Highness
b Your Majesty
c My Lord or My Lady
d Your Grace.

1 The Queen Mother

2 Prince Charles

3 The Duke of Kent

4 The Duke of Devonshire

5 Princess Margaret

6 A person whom you know to be black-listed arrives at the hotel, asking for accommodation. Which of the following phrases would be best to complete this phrase when refusing accommodation. I'm very sorry, but . . .

a . . . you are on our black list and I cannot offer you accommodation'
b . . . no accommodation is available'
c . . . the manager says you cannot stay'
d . . . all our rooms are full up.'

Below are four lettered fire extinguishers. Answer the following questions indicating which extinguisher should be used for the type of fire given.

a water
b CO_2
c vaporising liquid
d foam.

7 electric typewriter

8 deep fat fryer

9 waste-paper basket

10 bed

11 Match the type of extinguisher in List I with their colour codings in List II.

List I		List II	
A	water	1	cream
B	CO_2	2	blue
C	vaporising liquid	3	red
D	dry powder	4	grey/green
E	foam	5	black

a

A	B	C	D	E
3	5	4	2	1

b

A	B	C	D	E
3	5	1	4	2

c

A	B	C	D	E
2	4	3	1	5

d

A	B	C	D	E
2	4	1	5	3

12 A guest reports a suspicious-looking package, left in the hotel lounge. You think this may be a bomb. The Manager is at the cash and carry and you are the senior member of staff on duty. What action should you take before telephoning the police?

a Place it in a bucket of water
b Open it carefully to see what it contains
c Leave it where it is and evacuate the building
d Carry it carefully outside to the car park.

13 In any first aid emergency which is the correct order of treatment?

a bleeding, breathing, breakages
b breathing, bleeding, breakages
c breathing, breakages, bleeding
d bleeding, breakages, breathing.

14 There has been a fight in the bar and the manager has a nosebleed. What should you make him do?

a Hold his head back until the bleeding stops
b Hold a large ice cube on his forehead
c Hold his breath
d Hold his head slightly forward and pinch his nostrils.

15 A guest standing in reception feels faint. What should you do?

a Lay them on the floor and raise their feet
b Give them a brandy
c Suggest they go to their room and lie down
d Sit them on a chair and put their head between their knees.

Answer the following three questions, selecting the correct answer from the list below. Indicate your answer with the appropriate letter. Each letter may be used once, more than once or not at all.

a *Whitaker's Almanack*
b *Kelly's Directories*
c *Debrett's Peerage*
d *Pears Cyclopaedia*

In which of the reference books would you find the following information?

16 the date of Easter for the next two years

17 how to greet the Duke of Kent

18 the name of the President of the World Health Organisation.

Short-answer Questions (5 marks each)

19 What justification would you give to a guest who questions the value of completing the hotel's satisfaction form?

20 What action should be taken in the following situations?

(*a*) A guest is found in bed unconscious with an empty tablet bottle nearby
(*b*) A guest is found unconscious in the hotel swimming pool
(*c*) A guest has an epileptic fit.

21 Describe in detail the treatment you would give if a waiter's clothing caught on fire from a gueridon trolley.

Long-answer Questions (20 marks each)

22 A party of trainee receptionists from a local college visits your hotel. The manager has asked you to give them a short talk on deportment and personal appearance. Make notes on the topic areas you feel are important.

23 A new receptionist has just started, and you have been asked to give her guidelines for dealing with complaints. What advice would you give?

24 Describe ways in which the receptionist can help to sell the hotel's facilities.

25

Across

1 — agent (6)
3 Tub (4)
7 Polite behaviour (8)
8 — Share Index (2)
11 On time (8)
12 International sitting room (3)
13 Paying Guest (2)
14 3 single rooms in code (5)
15 Key to clear (1)
18 English oeuf! (3)
19, 20 Summary chart (4, 2)
21 American bonnet (4)
22 Planned method of work (6)

Down

1 Needed when handling complaints (4)
2 A zeal you should show (10)
4 Morning! (2)
5 Inns (6)
6 Study of guests' behaviour? (10)
9 What you must keep about the guests' details (3)
10 Luggage (3)
12 It's heard but not seen (6)
16 Exchange charge (4)
17 Accommodation (4)

Part Three
Advance Reservations

Multiple-choice Questions (1 mark each)

1 American plan is the term used to describe:

a full board
b half board
c bed and breakfast
d accommodation only.

2 An advanced reservation density chart should be used in conjunction with:

a guests' alphabetical index
b guests' history file
c booking diary
d room record cards.

3 Which symbol would indicate a twin bedded room on an advanced reservation chart?

a –
b =
c X
d :

4 A booking diary is best described as a book that indicates which:

a guests are arriving on a particular day
b rooms are to be taken off for special cleaning
c banqueting functions are to take place on a particular day
d guests have particular likes and dislikes.

5 A guest asking for communicating rooms would require:

a adjoining rooms
b adjoining rooms with connecting door
c adjoining rooms with an intercom
d opposite rooms, across a corridor.

6 If a prospective guest requests European plan terms, he requires:

a accommodation only
b bed and breakfast
c full board
d half board.

7 On a reservation chart the symbol X is normally used to indicate the following type of room:

a double bedded room
b twin bedded room
c single room
d studio room.

8 If an American asked for a cot, what would he require?

a a baby's crib
b a studio room
c a dog's basket
d an extra folding bed.

9 If the Reservations Manager asks you to 'walk' a guest, should you:

a tell him to go for a walk, whilst the room is made ready
b refuse him accommodation
c tell him you have deliberately overbooked and have not got a room
d find alternative accommodation in a similar hotel in the town?

10 Another term for half board is:

a American plan
b Continental plan
c European plan
d Modified American plan.

11 What charges do En Pension terms include?

a accommodation only
b room and breakfast
c room, breakfast and one other main meal
d room, breakfast, lunch, afternoon tea and dinner.

12 The term 'no show' is used to describe a guest that:

a arrived, hoping for a vacant room
b did not arrive on the appointed day
c cancelled his room in advance
d left without paying.

13 The International Hotel Telegraph Code is:

a a worldwide system to avoid confusion when making hotel reservations
b a worldwide system, used by telephonists to spell words clearly
c an international dialling code system
d an international code used by telephonists to pronounce words clearly.

14 Bed and breakfast terms can also be described as:

a American plan
b Continental plan
c European plan
d modified American plan.

15 When replying to a prospective guest's letter requesting details of accommodation and local amenities, the most effective procedure would be to send:

a a hotel brochure and local guide
b a compliment slip and local guide
c a specially written reply and hotel brochure
d a confirmation slip and local guide.

16 If a tour has been booked on demi-pension terms, what are the guests entitled to:

a room and breakfast
b room, breakfast, lunch, afternoon tea and dinner
c room, breakfast and one other main meal
d accommodation only.

17 If a guest has booked a room from one Saturday to the next, but does not arrive until the Monday, to find his room has been let, what is his legal position?

a He can demand that he is given the room for the rest of the week
b He can demand that alternative accommodation is found elsewhere
c He cannot demand anything, as the proprietor is entitled to assume that he is not coming at all
d He can sue the hotel for breach of contract.

18 Letters from guests regarding future accommodation are best filed:

a alphabetically
b by the date of arrival
c by the date of arrival, then alphabetically within the date
d according to the room number.

19 If a guest telephones for a single room and one is not available, the receptionist should:

a offer him a twin room
b offer him a double room
c suggest that he tries another hotel
d say that none are available and hang up.

20 Pair the terms in List I with their correct definitions in List II as they are applied in central reservations offices.

List I

A closed
B free sale
C no show
D walk in
E walk out

List II

1 There are vacancies for a particular date
2 The guest left without paying
3 A chance customer
4 The guest did not arrive
5 There are no vacancies left for a particular date.

a

A	B	C	D	E
5	1	4	3	2

b

A	B	C	D	E
5	2	4	3	1

c

A	B	C	D	E
2	5	3	1	4

d

A	B	C	D	E
2	4	1	5	3

21 If a guest has booked a week's accommodation and fails to arrive, but the hotelier is able to re-let the room for part of the week, the hotelier can claim compensation from the guest for:

a the whole week
b part of the week including meals
c part of the week for the accommodation element only
d nothing at all.

22 If a guest's contract for accommodation were frustrated through the hotel being burnt down, what would his legal rights be?

a none at all
b the right to the return of any deposit paid
c the right to claim full compensation
d the right to alternative accommodation.

23 If a person makes a reservation in a hotel whose brochure states that it is 5 minutes walk from the beach, and on arrival discovers that it is a good 15 minutes walk, the guest can:

a refuse to stay, but be liable to pay compensation to the hotel
b be made to carry out his contract with the hotel
c insist the hotel finds him alternative accommodation nearer to the beach
d refuse to stay and not be liable to pay any compensation to the hotel.

24 If a guest has confirmed a booking by post, when is the contract said to be complete?

a when the letter arrives at the hotel
b when the guest writes his letter
c when the guest posts his letter
d when the reservation is entered on the chart.

25 An 'invitation to treat' is best described as:

a the hotel confirming a reservation
b the hotel sending a brochure in response to a general enquiry
c the hotel sending details of accommodation available in answer to a specific enquiry and asking the guest to confirm
d the guest confirming a reservation.

Short-answer Questions (5 marks each)

26 (*a*) Study this conventional booking chart which is for next month. Can the following requests for accommodation be accepted?

(i) SB required for 4N from 2nd
(ii) DB required for 6N from 2nd
(iii) SB required for 6N from 6th

If so, briefly explain how it could be done.

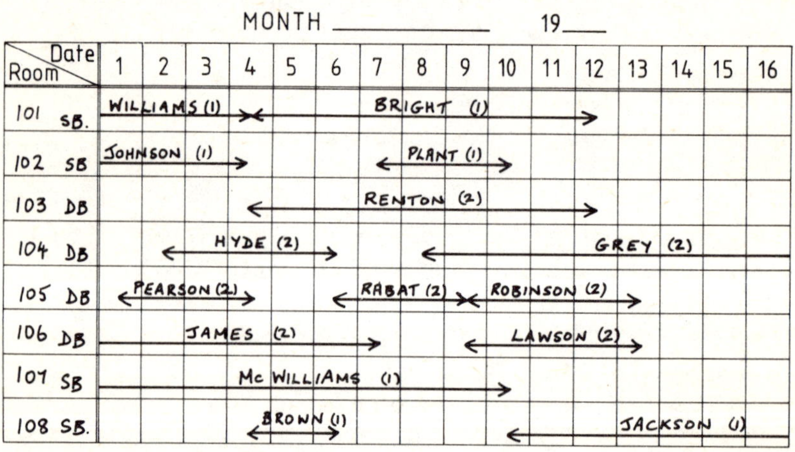

(*b*) List the problems which arise with the use of this sort of chart in a transient hotel.

27 Give a brief description of each of the following:

(*a*) release time
(*b*) centralised reservation office
(*c*) telex machine
(*d*) Prestel
(*e*) day let.

28 (*a*) Describe the purpose of the International Hotel Telegraph Code.

(*b*) Using the International Hotel Telegraph Code, translate the following:

(i) POGOK STOP AERO ALBA BAT BEST
(ii) ARAB KIND PLAIN BOX PASS RABAL
(iii) Arriving Friday night, staying several days, one room with one large bed and good view. Meet at station 15.00 hours
(iv) Cancel room tonight, arriving Sunday night, staying one night. One good-quality room with three beds.

Long-answer Questions (20 marks each)

29 Outline ways in which modern computer technology is being used for reserving hotel accommodation.

30 Design a comprehensive reservation form.

31 Describe the procedure for accepting a reservation by telephone from the moment the call is received to the filing of the information.

32 (*a*) Draw a density chart for the first two weeks of June and enter the following reservations listed in the table below. The hotel has five single rooms with private bathrooms, ten double rooms with private bathrooms, and six twin rooms with private bathrooms.

RESERVATIONS

Name	Type of room required	Terms	Date of arrival	Nights	Remarks
Mr Sandman	SB	AO	3 June	2	
Mrs Groves	SB	RB	4 June	4	Late arrival
Mr Briggs	TB	RB	1 June	2	Disabled
Mrs Fitzpatrick	TB	Inc	1 June	4	
Mr Ford	DB	AO	2 June	5	
Miss Morrison	SB	AO	10 June	4	
Mr Nutley	DB	RB	1 June	10	
Mrs Brown	SB	Inc	3 June	11	Deposit £50
Mr Smith	DB	Inc	5 June	7	
Mr Sandman	cancel SB on 12/4		3 June	2	
Mr Deer	SB	Inc	1 June	5	
Mr Oxford	2SB	RB	2 June	3	1 X Garage
Mr Mainwaring	6DB	RB	4 June	2	
Dr Sullivan	DB	Inc	1 June	7	Quiet room
Mr Ford	cancel DB on 6/5		2 June	5	

(*b*) Draw up two pages of the hotel reservations diary for 2 and 3 June.

Part Four
Reception Procedures

Multiple-choice Questions (1 mark each)

1 If a guest wishes to make a telephone call and the hotel is not equipped with meters, what service should the receptionist ask the operator for?

a STD call
b ADC call
c A and D call
d PBX call.

2 How long should guests' registration details be kept after arrival?

a six weeks
b two years
c six months
d one year.

3 What information is legally required from a British subject on registration?

a full name, address and telephone number
b full name, age and nationality
c full name, nationality and address
d full name, nationality and date of arrival.

4 An 'alien' for registration purposes refers to:

a an Australian citizen
b a foreign diplomat
c a Canadian citizen
d an American citizen.

5 Which of the following would be the most convenient system to use when registering a large tour party?

a individual forms
b loose-leaf system
c book register
d arrival and departure list.

6 What does the abbreviation IDD stand for?

a Internal Data Distribution

b International Direct Dialling
c Internal Direct Data
d International Datel Dialling.

7 From the following list, indicate the correct information which is required when a guest telephones to make a luncheon booking in the restaurant:

1 number of guests 2 name 3 time of arrival 4 telephone number 5 choice of dishes 6 date 7 method of payment

a 1, 2, 3, 4, 5, 6 and 7
b 1, 2, 3, 4, 5 and 6
c 1, 2, 3, 4 and 6
d 1, 2, 3 and 6.

8 What is the correct procedure to follow if a guest gives you some money in a sealed package for safe-keeping?

a Issue a safe deposit receipt and put the package in the safe
b Open the package, count the money and put it in the safe
c Tell them to leave it in their room and lock the door
d Put the package in the safe and tell them you will not be liable if it is stolen.

9 Under the Hotel Proprietors' Act and subject to certain conditions, the hotel proprietor can limit his liability for guests' belongings to:

a £100 per article
b £50 in total
c £50 per article
d £100 in total.

10 In which of the following circumstances can the hotel proprietor lose his limited liability for guests' property?

1 if the proprietor or his staff were negligent
2 if they failed to display the statutory notice
3 if the guest was negligent
4 if the goods were refused for safe deposit
5 if the goods were stolen whilst in the hotel's safe

a 1, 3, 4 and 5
b 2, 3, 4 and 5
c 1, 2, 3 and 4
d 1, 2, 4 and 5.

11 Which of the following Acts gives the hotel proprietor his right of sale of lien goods?

a Hotel Proprietors Act 1956
b Innkeepers Act 1878
c Offices, Shops and Railway Premises Act 1963
d Aliens Order 1953 and 1957

12 In the event of non-payment of a guest's account, the right of lien is the right to detain:

a the guest's property
b the guest's car
c the guest himself
d the guest's cheque-book.

13 What should you do with mail that you receive for guests that have not yet arrived?

a Mark it 'return to sender' and re-post it
b Place it in the letter rack under the room allocated
c Make a note in bookings diary and store the mail separately
d Keep it in Reception until the guest asks for it.

14 The function of a call sheet is to show which guests have:

a made telephone calls
b received telephone calls
c a message waiting for them
d requested calls, early morning tea and newspapers.

15 The letters GIT stand for:

a Guest In Transit
b Group In Transit
c Group Inclusive Terms
d Group Inclusive Tour.

16 Which of the following describe the function of a key card?

1 to record the serial number of the key
2 to remind the guest of the room number and room rate
3 to enable the guest to obtain his key from reception
4 to enable the guest to make charges to his account

a 1
b 2, 3 and 4
c 3
d 1, 2 and 3

17 The bed occupancy percentage is expressed as:

a $\dfrac{\text{Total sleeper capacity}}{\text{Number of sleepers}} \times \dfrac{100}{1}$

b $\dfrac{\text{Number of unsold sleeper spaces}}{\text{Number of sleeper spaces sold}} \times \dfrac{100}{1}$

c $\dfrac{\text{Number of sleepers}}{\text{Total sleeper capacity}} \times \dfrac{100}{1}$

d $\dfrac{\text{Number of sleeper spaces sold}}{\text{Number of unsold sleeper spaces}} \times \dfrac{100}{1}$

18 Disbursement is another term used to describe:

a a refund
b a safe deposit receipt
c a visitor's paid out
d a back-dated charge.

19 The main purpose of a reception board is to show:

a the status of each room at any moment in time
b the room rates
c the arrivals and departures
d the reservations.

20 Which of the following is the ideal position for the reception board?

a on the wall behind the reception desk, on view to the customer
b in the advance reservation office
c set into the reception desk, facing the receptionist
d in the reception manager's office.

21 For security reasons, the key rack should be placed:

a on the wall behind the reception desk, on view to the guest
b in the cashier's office
c behind the reception desk, out of the customer's view
d in the porter's lodge.

22 Match the colour coding, as used in the Whitney status system, in List I with the explanations in List II.

List I
A Yellow
B Clear
C Red

List II
1 Room vacant and ready
2 Room vacant, but not ready
3 Room just let

a

A	B	C
3	1	2

b

A	B	C
3	2	1

c

A	B	C
1	2	3

d

A	B	C
2	1	3

23 On a two-light electronic room status board, match the lights in List I with the explanations in List II.

List I A both lights off
B red light on
C green light on

List II 1 room ready to let
2 room occupied
3 room vacant, but not ready

a

A	B	C
3	1	2

b

A	B	C
2	3	1

c

A	B	C
1	2	3

d

A	B	C
3	2	1

24 Which of the following departments would benefit most from the installation of electronic room status boards?

1 kitchen 2 restaurant 3 reservations
4 reception 5 housekeeping 6 uniformed staff department
7 cashier

a 3, 4 and 5
b 1, 4 and 5
c 4, 5 and 7
d 4, 6 and 7

25 The purpose of the Tourism (Sleeping Accommodation Price Display) Order 1977 is to enable the guest to determine prices. These prices must be displayed:

a outside the hotel
b in the reception area
c in the guest's room
d in the lift.

26 What is the penalty for failing to comply with the Tourism (Sleeping Accommodation Price Display) Order 1977?

a £100
b £200
c £250
d £150

27 What does the abbreviation STD stand for

a Subscriber Time Dialling
b Standard Time Dialling
c Subscriber Trunk Dialling
d Standard Trunk Dialling.

28 The main purpose of the guests' history card is to keep a record of:

a regular guests and their particular requirements
b occupation and redecoration details of each room
c those guests not wanted in the hotel
d the charges the guest has accumulated on this stay to date.

29 When would a luggage pass or release slip be issued by the front office staff?

a on storage of the guest's luggage
b on return of the guest's luggage
c on settlement of the guest's bill
d on the departure of the guest.

30 Which of the following best describes the Uniqey system? It is a computerised:

a reservation system
b lock system
c accounting system
d room status system.

31 Match up the keys in List I with their correct definition in List II.

List I
A sub master
B master
C grand master

List II
1 opens and double locks all doors
2 opens all doors except those double-locked in one section or on one floor
3 opens all doors except those which are double-locked

a

A	B	C
2	1	3

b

A	B	C
2	3	1

c

A	B	C
1	2	3

d

A	B	C
3	2	1

32 For which of the following reasons can a receptionist *legally* refuse accommodation to a prospective guest?

1 He is not able or willing to pay
2 He is blacklisted
3 He is not in a fit state to be received
4 He has no luggage.

a 1 and 3
b 1 and 4
c 2 and 3
d 2 and 4

Answer the following three questions, selecting the correct answer from the list below. Indicate your answer with the appropriate letter. Each letter may be used more than once or not at all.

a VDU
b software
c floppy disc
d hardware

33 Which term is used to describe the program or set of instructions for the computer?

34 Which term is used to describe a type of data storage system?

35 Which term is used to describe the computer itself?

36 Roomwatch is a computerised system for:

a security
b room availability using Prestel
c room status
d early morning calls.

Short-answer Questions (5 marks each)

37 (*a*) Describe what you would say when answering a telephone call in reception:

(i) on an outside line
(ii) on an internal line.

(*b*) Describe what you would do if you were checking in a guest at reception and the telephone rang.

38 A lady at reception asks if she can see her brother Mr Banks who is a guest at the hotel. When you tell her that he is out, she asks if she can wait in his room. What action should you take?

Long-answer Questions (20 marks each)

39 Design a comprehensive individual registration form and explain the legislation and its requirements concerning registration.

40 Explain how electronic key systems can be used to replace conventional door key systems. Give the advantages and disadvantages of such a system.

41 A hotel has 50 bedrooms — 40 doubles and 10 singles. The following information shows the number of rooms sold over a period of one week.

	Mon.	Tue.	Wed.	Thur.	Fri.	Sat.	Sun.
Singles	4	5	8	10	8	4	2
Doubles (sold as doubles)	23	25	40	40	21	18	7
Doubles (sold as singles)	2	0	0	0	4	2	1

Calculate the following for *each* day and for the week in total:

(*a*) room occupancy
(*b*) sleeper occupancy
(*c*) double occupancy
(*d*) average room rate
(*e*) income occupancy.

The charge is £20 per person per night. A £25 charge is made for a double let as a single.

Part Five
Cashiers

Multiple-choice Questions (1 mark each)

1 A bill after a 10% service charge had been added is £27.72. Before the service charge, it was:

a £24.95
b £25.02
c £25.20
d £25.36.

2 Which of the following items on a visitor's bill are not subject to VAT?

1 visitors' disbursements
2 food taken in the restaurant
3 newspapers
4 telephone calls

a 1 and 2
b 1 and 3
c 3 and 4
d 2 and 4

3 How many weeks must a guest be in residence before VAT is charged on facilities only?

a 1 week
b 2 weeks
c 3 weeks
d 4 weeks

4 A guest's bill comes to £87.50 including a VPO for £5.00. What will be the final amount after the addition of 15% VAT and 10% service?

a £109.36
b £109.94
c £110.69
d £104.94.

5 A customer's bill comes to £65.00 which includes 15% VAT and $12\frac{1}{2}$% service charge. What was the total before VAT and service were added?

a $£47.12\frac{1}{2}$
b £48.34
c £49.84
d £50.24.

6 A guest has been staying for five weeks, and has been charged £20.00 per week for accommodation. How much will he now owe in total, including VAT at 15%? (Assume 'facilities' are worth 20% of the weekly accommodation charge.)

a £112.15
b £112.60
c £115.00
d £138.00.

Answer the following three questions, selecting the correct currency from the list below. Indicate your answer with the appropriate letter.

a riyal
b dinar
c schilling
d punt

7 What is the currency of Austria?

8 What is the currency of Saudi Arabia?

9 What is the currency of Eire?

Answer the following three questions, selecting the correct currency from the list below. Indicate your answer with the appropriate letter.

a peseta
b lira
c Deutsche Mark
d guilder

10 What is the currency of the Netherlands?

11 What is the currency of West Germany?

12 What is the currency of Italy?

13 A French visitor wishes to obtain £24 sterling. How many francs must you as cashier receive if the exchange rate is 9.5 francs to the pound?

a 188 francs
b 190 francs
c 220 francs
d 228 francs.

14 A Japanese guest gives you 16 000 yen in payment of a £25 bill. How much change should he receive if the exchange rate is 520 yen to the pound?

a £5.65
b £5.67
c £5.75
d £5.77.

15 An Italian tourist wishes to exchange 5 000 lire. How many pounds should you give him if the exchange rate is 1 900 lire to the pound?

a £2.63
b £2.65
c £2.73
d £2.75.

16 What should you give as change to an American businessman who tenders a $1 000 traveller's cheque in settlement of a £400 account? (The exchange rate is $2.30 to the £.)

a $80
b £34.78
c £13.80
d $80 in traveller's cheques.

17 The cost of 1 000 NCR bills is £61.00. What net amount is payable if we receive a 20% trade discount and a 5% cash discount?

a £45.75
b £46.36
c £48.41
d £48.80.

18 A new oven range costs £750. How much would a hotel save if it received a 25% trade discount and a 3% cash discount?

a £187.50
b £194.44½
c £204.37½
d £210.00

19 The 15% service charge received for June was £895.00. How much would the cashier receive if she was entitled to a 12% share?

a £107.40
b £109.20
c £120.00
d £140.70.

20 If 250 kg of potatoes cost £25.00, what would 750 grams cost?

a $2\frac{1}{2}$p
b $7\frac{1}{2}$p
c 25p
d 75p.

21 If a guest presents you with a cheque already signed in settlement of an account, what should you do?

a Accept it as it is
b Ask them to sign again on the reverse
c Refuse to accept it
d Ask them to write another cheque out.

22 If you receive a 'post-dated' cheque by mail, the date on the cheque would be for:

a some time in the future
b some time in the past
c today's date
d the date it was posted.

23 What information from the cheque card is written on the reverse of the cheque to guarantee payment?

a the bank code number
b the date of expiry
c the guest's signature
d the card number

24 Match the terms used for cheques in List I with their explanations in List II.

List I
A payee
B drawer
C drawee

List II
1 person writing the cheque
2 account holder's bank
3 person the cheque is made out to

a

A	B	C
3	2	1

b

A	B	C
1	2	3

c

A	B	C
2	1	3

d

A	B	C
3	1	2

25 How should you endorse a cheque?

a Write 'pay cash' on the front
b Write your address on the back
c Sign your name on the front
d Sign your name on the back.

26 After what period from the date shown on the cheque will the bank refuse to clear it?

a 3 months
b 6 months
c 9 months
d 12 months.

27 A cheque that has been crossed indicates that:

a it must be paid through a bank account
b it can be cashed over a bank counter
c it cannot be endorsed to another person
d it requires special clearance.

28 A correction on a cheque should be validated by:

a the payee's initials
b the drawer's signature
c the drawer's initials
d the payee's signature.

29 A cheque crossed 'a/c payee' indicates that:

a it must be cashed at the payee's bank
b it can only be paid into the drawer's bank account
c it can only be paid into the presenter's bank account
d it can only be paid into the payee's bank account.

30 When telephoning a bank to confirm the validity of a cheque presented without a cheque card, you should ask for:

a an authorisation number
b a special clearance
c a banker's reference
d a statement.

31 The initials RD on a cheque returned from the bank mean:

a refer to deceased
b reliability doubtful
c refer to drawer
d regular debtor.

32 Which of the following coins are no longer legal tender?

1 1d
2 1/-
3 6d
4 2/-
5 2/6
6 $\frac{1}{2}$d

a 1, 3, 5 and 6
b 2, 3, 4 and 5
c 1, 2, 3, 4, 5 and 6
d 1, 5 and 6

33 What is the legal maximum for accepting bronze coins (2p, 1p, $\frac{1}{2}$p)?

a 10p
b 20p
c 25p
d £5.

34 How many cupro-nickel coins (10p, 5p) can you legally accept?

a £5 worth
b £10 worth
c £15 worth
d £20 worth.

35 Up to what value are 50p pieces legal tender?

a £5
b £10
c £15
d £20.

36 How long are traveller's cheques usually valid for?

a 6 months
b 1 year
c 5 years
d no time limit

37 Which of the following provides the best proof of identity when accepting a traveller's cheque from a foreign guest?

a the guest's passport
b the guest's cheque card
c the guest's driving licence
d the guest's credit card

38 Which of the following credit cards may also be used as a bank cheque card?

a Access
b Diners Club
c American Express
d Barclaycard Visa

39 Which of the following groups of credit cards are all issued free of charge to the client?

a Barclaycard Visa, Access, American Express
b Mastercharge, Diners Club, Carte Blanche
c American Express, Diners Club, Carte Blanche
d Access, Barclaycard Visa, Mastercharge.

40 What is the correct procedure to follow if you were presented with a credit card which you found was on your stop list?

a Telephone the authorisation centre
b Telephone the police
c Tear up the card
d Ask for another form of payment.

41 Arrange the following actions in the correct order of sequence for accepting payment by credit card before you compare the signatures.

1 Print card details
2 Check that the hotel accepts that kind of card
3 Prepare sales voucher
4 Ask customer to sign.

a 1, 2, 3 and 4
b 2, 1, 3 and 4
c 2, 4, 1 and 3
d 2, 1, 4 and 3

42 What is the machine called which transfers details from the credit card on to the sales voucher?

a inprinter
b enprinter
c imprinter
d emprinter

43 Which of the following best describes a credit card floor limit?

a a limit set for the hotel by the credit card company, above which authorisation must be obtained
b a limit set for the guest by the credit card company, above which authorisation must be obtained

c an upper limit set by the hotel for each credit card above which authorisation must be obtained from the manager
d a daily limit set by the hotel for each credit card, above which authorisation must be obtained from the manager.

44 If the hotel's High Street bank has set the rate of exchange at \$2.50 to the £, at which rate should the hotel accept payment in dollars?

a \$2.50
b \$2.55
c \$2.45
d \$2.40.

45 If a guest has booked through a travel agent, when should you ask him for his copy of the voucher?

a when he pays his bill
b when he sends his confirmation
c one week in advance
d on arrival at the hotel.

Short-answer Questions (5 marks each)

46 Draw a petty cash voucher and illustrate how it should be completed to show a payment for Chef's taxi fare of £2.50. Use today's date.

47 Define the purpose of a float and state the factors which determine its size.

48 Define the 'build and say' method of giving change. Give an example.

49 Show diagrammatically the 'clearance of a cheque' through the banking system.

50 Describe the difference between a bank cheque card and a credit card.

Long-answer Questions (20 marks each)

51 Discuss the advantages and disadvantages to the hotel of settlement of guests' bills by ledger accounts.

52 Draw the analysed petty cash book of the Moderna Hotel which is kept on the Imprest system. On Aug 1, 19—, the balance was £20. Post the following transactions.

Voucher No	Date	Details	Amount
32	Aug 1	Paid for postage stamps	£6.50
33	Aug 2	Paid for guest's dry cleaning Room 127 Mr. Blackledge	£2.25
34	Aug 3	Paid for waitresses' taxi	£1.50
35	Aug 4	Paid for guest's taxi Room 316 Miss Whitlock	£5.30
36	Aug 4	Paid for bread Bapat the Baker	£2.00
37	Aug 5	Paid for typing paper	£0.75
38	Aug 7	Paid for COD parcel for Room 321 Mr Davey	£0.90

Balance the week's transactions.

53 Draw a diagram of a cheque card and list the points to be verified when accepting payment by cheque with a cheque card.

54 Describe how the cashier's takings should be prepared for paying into the bank.

Part Six
Book Keeping

Multiple-choice Questions (1 mark each)

Indicate in which section of the ledger the following accounts would be found by choosing the appropriate letter **a**, **b**, **c**, or **d**. Each letter may be used once, twice, or not at all.

a purchases ledger
b sales ledger
c general ledger/real account
d general ledger/nominal account.

1 wages account

2 T Tripe who supplies the hotel with meat

3 furniture account

4 rates account

5 Mr. Black, who owes the hotel £900 for a wedding reception

6 The book which shows analysed daily totals of tabular ledger sheets and the business done for each week and month is called:

a the accounts ledger
b the journal
c the allowances book
d the summary book.

Below are four documents. Indicate by choosing their letter (**a, b, c, d**) the answer to the following questions. Each document may be used once, more than once, or not at all.

a credit note
b invoice
c statement
d delivery note.

7 Which document shows the balance due to the supplier at the end of the month?

8 Which document does not show any prices or amount owing?

9 Which document shows a detailed description of the goods supplied and the amount due?

10 Which document would show the trade discount given?

11 Which document would be issued by the supplier for the return of faulty or substandard goods?

Below are four tax forms. Indicate by choosing their letter **(a, b, c, d)** the answers to the following questions. Each form may be used once, more than once or not at all.

a P11
b P35
c P45
d P60.

12 Which form is given to an employee on leaving his job?

13 Which form is used by the employer for each employee to show his weekly or monthly tax deductions?

14 Which form is used by the employer for his annual return to the Collector of Taxes?

15 Which form is given to each employee at the end of the financial year to show his total pay and tax deductions?

16 Which form indicates a new employee's tax code?

Short-answer Questions (5 marks each)

17 Draw up a sales ledger account for the Opus Operatic Society with a balance brought forward of £256.67 and a page from the cash book. Enter the cost of their luncheon for today of £87.59 and enter a cash payment of £96.42. Balance the ledger account.

18 Explain the difference between a cash discount and a trade discount.

19 Explain how you would show a charge on the tabular ledger of £10 for wine which should have been posted to Mr Quick in Room 17 yesterday.

20 Describe how the guests' tabular ledger forms part of the hotel's double-entry system by explaining how double entry is completed for:

(*a*) charges to the visitor
(*b*) cash received from visitors
(*c*) VPOs
(*d*) allowances.

21 Explain the function of the following keys on a mechanical guests' accounting machine:

(*a*) shift key
(*b*) X key
(*c*) Z key.

22 Calculate the selling price of the following dishes to be served in the hotel's restaurant.

	Food cost	*Gross profit (%) required*
(*a*)	25p	60%
(*b*)	39p	70%
(*c*)	£1.63	57%
(*d*)	98p	68%
(*e*)	62p	55%

23 Calculate the gross profit % from the following information.

	Food cost	*Selling price*
(*a*)	92p	£2.30
(*b*)	£1.95	£6.00
(*c*)	£1.30	£3.95
(*d*)	67p	£1.45
(*e*)	£2.50	£8.00

Long-answer Questions (20 marks each)

24 (*a*) Draw up a cash analysis of the following net wages to enable you to prepare these wage packets.

Mrs Renton	£46.98
Mrs Flood	£116.43
Mr Gamble	£37.02
Miss Bird	£78.16
Mr Robinson	£12.68

(*b*) Explain the function of the following:

(i) personal tax code
(ii) tax table A
(iii) tax table B.

25 (*a*) What is the purpose of balancing the tabular ledger at the end of the day?

(*b*) Which types of error are *not* revealed by balancing? Give an example of each indicating how they may be detected.

26 Two dinners costing, in total, £15.86 were posted yesterday to room 23 instead of room 33 on the tabular ledger.

(*a*) Explain how you would show the correction.

(*b*) Illustrate your answer by drawing an analysed page in the allowances book.

(*c*) Briefly state the purpose of the allowances book.

27 Outline the advantages of installing an electronic billing machine. List the factors which need to be considered when purchasing such a machine.

The following three questions are to be answered on a tabular ledger sheet.

28 **Tariff for the Ship Inn**

Room and breakfast	£14.00 (inc. of bft £2.00) per person
Inclusive terms	£24.00 (inc. of board £12.00) per person
Private bathroom	£8.00 per room per night
Early morning tea	40p per person
Morning coffee	60p per person
Table d'hôte lunch	£4.00 per person
Meal beverage	40p extra per person

(Inclusive terms include room, breakfast, lunch, afternoon tea and dinner.)

Guests in Residence

Type	*Terms*	*Room*	*Name*	*Amount b/f*
DB	INC.	14	Mr & Mrs B West	£116.72
SB	R & B	20	Mr P Parker	£60.44
SB	R & B	25	Miss R Rose	£14.00
S	INC.	31	Mr R Ashmore	£28.00
TW	R & B	32	Mr & Mrs J Webb	£49.44

List of Transactions

0730	EMT to all residents. Newspapers: Rm 31 — 20p, Rm 14 — £1.20, Rm 20 — 40p
0745	Telephone calls: Rm 14 — £1.20; Rm 20 — £1.80; Rm 25 — 80p, Rm 31 — 80p, Rm 32 — £2.20.
0800	Rm 31 checks out and pays in cash.
0815	Rm 20 VPO flowers £6.00.
0830	Chance breakfasts £34.00.
0845	Rm 14 checks out and pays account by cheque (advance deposit — £20.00).
0930	Rm 32 pays £40.00 in cash on account.
1030	Chance telephones £9.80.
1100	Morning coffee to all residents.

1130 Chance coffee £7.00.
1215 Arrival: Mr and Mrs Q Lawley, given Rm 14 on inclusive terms.
1230–1400 Luncheons
Rm 20 £4.00, 1 coffee, beer 56p
Rm 25 £4.00, wine £2.24
Rm 32 £8.00, coffee 80p, brandy £3, cigar £1.00
Rm 14 2 luncheons, coffee 80p, minerals 60p
Chance: £100.80, beverages £8.40, wines £19.80, spirits £27.20, minerals 44p, tobacco £4.56.
1415 Rm 20 asks to be changed to Rm 31.
1430 Allowances and adjustments for yesterday's tab.: Rm 32 allowed 80p EMT, Rm 25 undercharged for dinner £2.00.
1500 Rotary Club luncheon. 55 covers at £8.40 each (inc. of 40p per person for hire of room), wines £96.00, liqueurs £60.00, cigars £30.00. Account to be sent to treasurer of the club.
1515 Lounge bar pays in £199.30 for spirits and liqueurs and £21.60 for beers.

Balance and reconcile all totals as if it was the end of the day's business.

29 **Tariff for the Royal Esplanade Hotel**

European plan	£30.00 per person per night
Continental plan	£35.00 per person per night (inc. bft £5.00)
American plan	£48.00 per person per night (inc. board £18.00)
EMT	£0.50 per person
Breakfast	£5.00 per person
Morning coffee	£0.65 per person
Luncheon	£7.55 per person
Afternoon tea	£1.25 per person
Dinner	£10.30 per person
After-meal beverage	£0.50 per person
Private bathroom	£5.00 per room per night

All prices are inclusive of service charge and VAT.
Full board includes room, breakfast, lunch, afternoon tea and dinner.

Balance and reconcile all totals, as if at the end of the day's business.

Guests in Residence

Room	*Type*	*Name*	*Amount b/f*	*Terms*
101	DB	Mr & Mrs Baldwin	£201.63	EP
209	TB	Major & Mrs Philpott	£62.29	CP
210	T	Mr & Mrs Capland	£16.92 credit	CP
304	DB	Mr & Mrs Cowley	£36.39	AP
305	SB	Miss White	£49.61	CP
309	S	Mr Crabtree	£111.01	EP

List of Transactions

0730 EMT to all residents.
0900 Breakfast served to all residents.
0930 Telephone calls: Rm 309 – 62p, Rm 210 – 75p.
0945 VPO: Rm 304 – £6.56 Theatre tickets.
1015 Departures: Rm 209 pays cash less an advance deposit of £100.
1020 Allowances and adjustments for errors in yesterday's tab. Rm 304 charged £10.00 for breakfast instead of Rm 101.
1030 Rm 305 pays £150 cash on account.
1050 Morning coffee to all residents.
1130 Chance morning coffees: 5.
1400 Lunches: Rms 101, 210, 309, 304. All those taking lunch have coffee after the meal. Wines: Rm 101 – £6.36, Rm 309 £9.88. Tobacco Rm 304 – £1.25. Drinks: Rm 304 – 1pt beer 70p, Rm 309 – brandies £1.67.
Chance lunches: 36, wines £52.51, tobacco £5.93.
1430 Arrivals: Mr & Mrs Jackson are given Rm 209, they pay for 5 nights in advance by cheque. Terms: American plan.
Mr Graham, Rm 102 SB. Terms: European plan.
1500 Private function: Pickard School of Motoring lunch. 69 covers at £5.95, wines £25.00, room hire £5.00, cash wines £16.52. Account to ledger; folio P/16s.
1600 All residents take afternoon tea.
Chance teas: 36 (two teas paid by American Express credit card).
2030 All residents have dinner. Wines: Rm 209 – £16.01, Rm 304 – £4.25. After-meal beverages Rm 209 and Rm 102.
2230 Cocktail bar pays in £16.52 for beers, £25.95 for spirits and liqueurs and £12.76 for tobacco.

30 Tariff for the Amesbury Arms Hotel

Room and breakfast	£25.50 (inc. of bft £2.50) per person
Inclusive terms	£35.00 (inc. of board £15.00) per person
Private bathroom	£5.00 per room per night
Early morning tea	£0.50 per person
Breakfast	£2.50 per person
Morning coffee	£0.60 per person
Luncheon (table d'hôte)	£5.75 per person
After-meal beverage	£0.55 per person

NB Inclusive terms cover room, breakfast, luncheon, afternoon tea and dinner only.
All prices inclusive of service and VAT.

Guests in Residence

Type	*Terms*	*Room*	*Name*	*Amount b/f*
DB	R & B	201	Mr & Mrs Gutteridge	£193.07
TB	INC.	309	Capt & Mrs Stevens	£64.72
T	R & B	310	Mr & Mrs Briggs	£20.27CR
DB	INC.	404	Mr & Mrs Williams	£53.48
SB	R & B	405	Miss Bapat	£42.71
S	INC.	409	Mr Davey	£114.50

List of Transactions

0730 EMT to all residents.
Newspapers: Rm 309 — 15p, Rm 404 — 25p, Rm 405 — 30p.

0745 Telephone calls: Rm 409 — £1.25, Rm 201 — 16p, Rm 404 — 32p.

0800 Allowances and adjustments for errors in yesterday's tab: Rm 201 — omission of £6.50 wine charge. Rm 409 — charged £5.75 for luncheon instead of Rm 405.

0900 All residents have breakfast.
Chance breakfasts: 5.

0930 Departures: Rm 201 pays by Access credit card, less an amount of £100 received as an advance deposit.
Rm 405 pays in full by cash.

1000 Rm 409 moves to Rm 405.
Rm 310 pays £75 on account.

1100 All residents are served with morning coffee.
Chance morning coffee: 16.

1130 Arrival: Mr Sweetland is given Rm 409 on inclusive terms and pays for seven nights in advance by cash.

1300 Luncheons: Rm 309 — 2 luncheons, one coffee, one brandy — 90p. Rm 310 — 2 luncheons, 2 coffees, wine £5.92. Rm 405 — one guest for luncheon, wine £10.39, cigars £2.50, 2 glasses of port £1.20.
Chance luncheons: £69.00, wine £20.51, coffees £5.50.
Private luncheon in Mason Suite for Alpha Aero Club: Room hire £5.00, beers £25, 20 luncheons at £7.50 inclusive of coffee at 55p. Cash wines £15.72. Account to be sent to Club Chairman. (A/2)

1400 Arrival; Whistle Stop Tours — 16 persons — 8 double rooms 501–508 for one night only. Special room and breakfast rate of £20 per person (inclusive of breakfast £2.50) account to ledger. (W/1)

Balance and reconcile all totals as if it was the end of the day's business.

Answers

PART ONE: HOTEL ORGANISATION

Multiple-choice questions

1 c	2 a	3 c	4 b
5 a	6 c	7 d	8 b
9 b	10 c	11 a	12 a
13 c	14 c	15 a	16 b
17 a	18 a	19 d	20 c
21 b	22 d	23 b	24 c
25 a	26 d	27 a	28 d
29 b	30 c	31 d	32 a
33 b			

Short-answer Questions

34 (*a*) Corkage is a charge made to the guest for bringing their own bottle of alcoholic beverage for consumption on the premises.

(*b*) *Mise en place* is preparing the restaurant and bar for service.

(*c*) A gueridon is a trolley from which dishes are prepared, finished off or served in the restaurant.

(*d*) A dumb waiter is a small food lift.

(*e*) An aboyeur is the member of the kitchen staff who calls out the waiters' orders at the hot plate.

(*f*) A demi-tasse is a small coffee cup with a volume of $2\frac{1}{2}$fl. oz.

35 *A place setting for a table d'hôte menu*

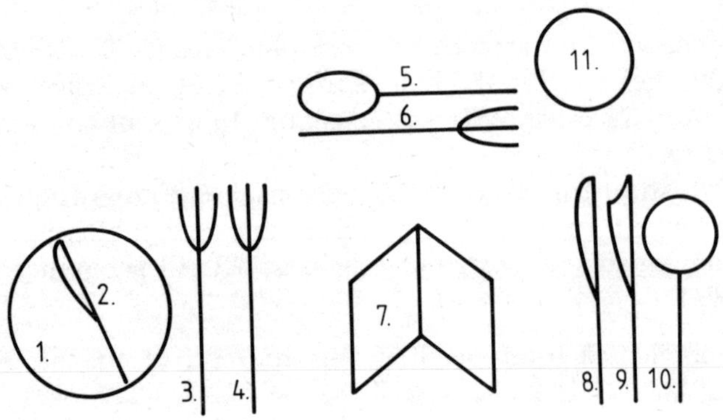

1 side plate
2 side knife
3 fish fork
4 joint fork
5 dessert spoon
6 dessert fork
7 napkin
8 joint knife
9 fish knife
10 soup spoon
11 glass

36 *An early morning tea tray for one*

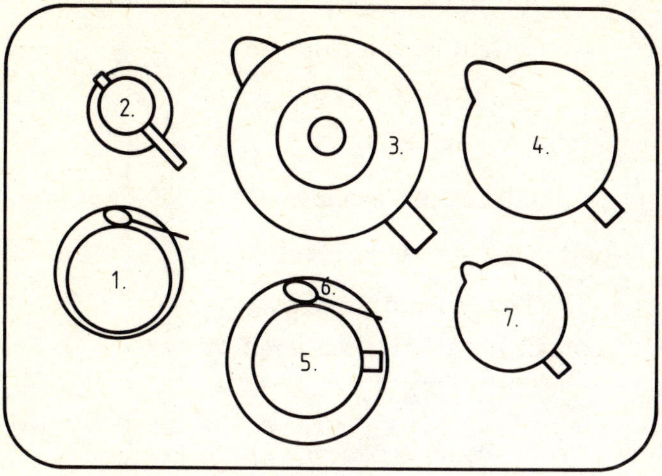

1 sugar bowl
2 slop basin and tea strainer
3 tea pot
4 hot water jug
5 tea cup and saucer
6 tea spoon
7 milk jug

37 (*a*) A choice from each of the following courses:

Fruit juice, Cereal, Stewed fruit
Grilled herrings, Poached smoked haddock, Kedgeree
Eggs: boiled, poached, fried, scrambled, omelettes
Bacon, Sausages
Tomatoes, Mushrooms, Sauté Potatoes
Toast, Bread, Rolls, Preserves
Tea or Coffee

(*b*) Rolls, Croissants, Toast, Preserves, Coffee or Tea

38 (*a*) Paris goblet: wine, spirits, aperitifs, mineral water, fruit juices
(*b*) Elgin: sherry
(*c*) Tulip: champagne, other wines
(*d*) Hock: wine from the Rhine region of Germany
(*e*) Brandy balloon: brandy

39

Jus de tomate
Oeuf mayonnaise
Consommé royale

★ ★ ★

Filet de plie meunière

★ ★ ★

Poulet sauté chasseur
Côte de boeuf rôtie, sauce raifort

★ ★ ★

Pommes rôties
Pommes duchesse
Choux de Bruxelles
Carottes au beurre

★ ★ ★

Bavarois au chocolat
Crêpes au citron
Glace vanille

★ ★ ★

Café

40 *Restaurant bookings diary*

Day: FRIDAY			Date: 21st OCTOBER			Meal: LUNCHEON
Name	Tel. No.	Time	No. of Covers	Running Total	Special Requirements	Table No. (for Rest. use)
SMITH	27834	12·30	4	4	—	
POOLE	38426	12·30	3	7	vegetarian meal for one.	
JONES	23268	12·45	2	9	Window table.	

41 Possible answers are:

Chef garde manger — Larder chef. Prepares raw meat, poultry and game and cold dishes.
Chef saucier — Sauce chef. Prepares entrées and their sauces.
Chef rôtisseur — Roast chef. Prepares roasts, grills and deep fried dishes.
Chef poissonier — Fish chef. Prepares all fish dishes except for deep fried or grilled fish.
Chef entremettier — Vegetable chef. Prepares all vegetables, egg and farinaceous dishes.
Chef potager — Soup chef. Prepares soups.
Chef pâtissier — Pastry chef. Prepares all pastry, sweets, ice cream and petits fours.

42 A bin card tells the storekeeper exactly how much he has in stock at any moment of time. It shows the minimum stock so that he can reorder and the maximum stock to prevent overstocking and, therefore, deterioration.

A bin card

Item .... Unit			Bin No. .... Max. stock .... Min. stock ....
Date	Received	Issued	Balance

43 All staff must be aware that lost property must be handed to the person who is in charge of it. A record must be kept of: a description of the article; who found it; when and where it was found. It is advisable to report valuable finds to the police. Every effort must be made to return the item to the rightful owner, and the claimant ought to be able to prove to the hotel's satisfaction that they are the rightful owner.
After a reasonable time period, e.g. 6 months, if the item is not claimed, it may possibly be offered to the person who found it.
NB. If no effort is made to trace the rightful owner, this may be interpreted as theft.

44 (*a*) Société des Clefs d'Or is an international society of Hall Porters. Each member wears a badge of two gold crossed keys.

(*b*) A linkman or doorman greets guests from their car or taxi and escorts them to reception.

(*c*) A valet takes care of guests' clothes, unpacking and packing, pressing and laundering or cleaning them as necessary.

(*d*) The lodge is the area of the reception desk nearest to the hotel entrance to monitor the entrance and exit of visitors. The luggage room is normally situated behind this area.

(*e*) A luggage pass is issued by the cashier when a guest has settled his account. This informs the porter that the guest's luggage may be released in exchange for the pass.

(*f*) The watchman's time clock is carried by the night porter whilst patrolling around the hotel. At selected points, keys which are chained to the wall are inserted into the clock which records on an audit roll the time. This roll can be checked by the manager to ensure the hotel has been regularly patrolled throughout the night.

45 (*a*) A bedboard is a wooden board placed between the mattress and the base of the bed to give additional support to back sufferers.

(*b*) The occupancy list, sleepers list or room status report indicates the number of sleepers in each room for the previous night.

(*c*) The linen room contains a store of clean linen and facilities for repairing it. It may also deal with staff uniforms and guests' personal laundry.

(*d*) OOO denotes that a room is out of order for deep cleaning or repairs.

(*e*) A studio room provides extra space during the day by pushing the beds under fixed back rests. Therefore, the room may be used as a lounge or let as a day-let for hospitality.

Long-answer Questions

46 *Banqueting memorandum*

Type of function: . . . . Room(s): . . . . Name of organiser: . . . . Address: . . . . Telephone:	Date of function: . . . . Time – Arrive: . . . . – Meal service: . . . . – Depart: . . . .
Menu	No. of covers: . . . .
Wines:	Bar(s): Occasional licence no.: . . . .
Extras: Cigars/cigarettes: . . . . Toastmaster: . . . . Printing: . . . . Cloakroom:	 Flowers: . . . . Changing room: . . . . Band: . . . . Audio equipment: . . . .
Account details: (cash, credit, deposit)	
Booked on (date):	Booked by: . . . .
Confirmation received:	
Copies to: Kitchen: . . . . . . Restaurant: . . . . . . Banqueting manager: . . . . . . Housekeeper: . . . . . . Porter: . . . . . . Cellar man:	

47 *Conference/exhibition booking form*

Type of function: . . . . Date of function: . . . .

Room(s): . . . . Time – Arrive/reception: . . . .

Name of organiser: . . . . – Meeting: . . . .

Address: . . . . – Depart: . . . .

. . . .

Telephone: . . . . No. of delegates: . . . .

Room hire charges: . . . .

Room(s): . . . . . . *Nos.:* . . . . . . *Audio visual:*

Seating – Theatre: . . . . Blackboard: . . . . Flipchart: . . . .

– Schoolroom: . . . . O.H.P.: . . . Screen: . . . .

– Boardroom: . . . . Cine 8mm: . . . 16mm: . . . 32mm: . . .

– Exhibition booths: . . . . Video: . . . Audiotape: . . . .

Microphone(s): . . . Speakers: . . . .

Lectern(s): . . . . Signs: . . . .

Special requirements:

(Electrical/Garage/Security/Press/Advertising/Photographer/Translator)

Service of food and drinks

Bars: . . . . Cash/credit Occasional licence: . . . .

Morning coffee: Time: . . . . No. . . . . Room: . . . . . Charge: . . . . .

Lunch (menu): Time: . . . . No. . . . . Room: . . . . . Charge: . . . . .

Afternoon tea: Time: . . . . No. . . . . Room: . . . . . Charge: . . . . .

Dinner (menu): Time: . . . . No. . . . . Room: . . . . . Charge: . . . . .

Account details: (Cash, credit, deposit)

Booked on (date): . . . . Booked by: . . . .

Confirmation received: . . . .

Copies to: Function manager: . . . . . Kitchen: . . . . . House porters: . . . . .

Restaurant: . . . . Housekeeper: . . . .

48 It is best to be systematic, working clockwise or anticlockwise around the room. The following points should be noted:

- Lights — bulbs working
- Wardrobe — clean and empty
- Dressing table — polished, drawers empty, mirror, stationery
- Curtains — easily drawn
- Bed(s) — made with clean linen
- Bedside console — TV, radio, alarm, telephone etc. in working order
- Carpet — vacuumed
- Bathroom — bath, wash basin, toilet, bidet, floor clean. Clean towels, fresh soap and complimentary items
- Door — fire notice.

49

1 A	C	2 C	O	3 M	M	O	D	4 A	T	5 I	O	6 N
M	■	O	■	I	■	■	■	R	■	R	■	E
E	■	N	■	N	■	7 S	E	R	V	I	C	E
8 R	E	C	E	I	P	T	■	I	■	S	■	D
I	■	I	■	■	■	O	■	V	■	■	■	■
9 C	H	E	F	10 A	B	O	Y	E	11 U	12 R	■	13 A
A	■	K	■	R	■	L	■	■	14 N	U	T	S
N	■	G	■	E	■	■	■	15 A	I	M	■	S
16 P	R	E	P	A	Y	17 M	E	N	T	■	■	I
L	■	S	■	L	■	E	■	I	■	18 C	O	S
A	■	■	19 M	A	G	N	U	M	■	O	■	T
N	■	■	■	L	■	U	■	20 A	N	K	L	E
■	21 A	C	C	E	S	S	■	L	■	E	■	D

50 (*a*) Three areas: (i) guests, (ii) staff, (iii) the hotel itself.

(i) Guests benefit by:

- smoothly run hotel
- good service
- good communications.

(ii) Staff benefit by:

- good working relations
- high morale and motivation
- good communications.

(iii) Hotel benefits by:

- repeat business because of efficient, friendly image
- low staff turnover
- good communications
- purchasing and forecasting
- staff planning
- maximum occupancy.

(*b*) Examples where co-operation is important between front office and each of the other hotel departments:

(i) *House keeping*

- allocation of rooms (consider: arrivals, A & D list, rooms out of order, room status, group bookings)
- special requests (consider: VIPs, Z beds (rollaways), bed-boards, extra bedding and linen, flowers)
- lost property
- staff uniforms
- guests' laundry/dry cleaning
- housekeeper's occupancy report
- early morning tea/calls/newspapers
- functions

(ii) *Uniformed Staff*

- security
- issue of keys
- arrivals and departures (consider: luggage/luggage passes, groups and tours, car parking, night arrivals)
- functions
- theatre tickets/car hire, etc.
- messages/paging/guests' mail

(iii) *Kitchen*

- occupancy forecasts (consider the A & D list)
- functions (consider the function list)
- special requests (consider diets, late suppers, early break-fasts)
- staff meals
- food orders
- COD payments
- petty cash purchases

(iv) *Restaurant*

- occupancy forecasts, functions, special requests — as for kitchen
- special requests (consider: window seats/sea views)
- room service

(v) *Control and Accounts Office*

- careful preparation of accounts
- accurate information (consider: cash reports, cash summaries, ledger accounts)
- credit control (consider walk outs)

(vi) *Maintenance*

- prompt reports of faults
- rooms out of order for redecoration, etc.

(vii) *Sales Department*

- feedback of occupancy
- discounted and complimentary rooms
- reservation forecasts

PART TWO: THE HOTEL RECEPTIONIST

Multiple-choice Questions

1 b	2 a	3 a	4 d
5 a	6 b	7 b	8 d
9 a	10 a	11 a	12 c
13 b	14 d	15 d	16 a
17 c	18 d		

Short-answer Questions

19 (*a*) It gives hotel feedback on its provision of facilities, e.g. food and beverage service, accommodation

(*b*) It highlights areas which are good and, more important, those which are not coming up to guests' expectations

(*c*) It gives the hotel a profile of the guest for future planning so that the customers' needs might be met more effectively.

20 (*a*) Call an ambulance. Give the bottle to the ambulancemen so that doctors can give the correct treatment

(*b*) Retrieve the guest from the pool. Give mouth-to-mouth resuscitation by laying the guest on his back, tilting his head back to give clear passage to lungs, holding his nose and blowing into his mouth, and watching his chest rise — which should take place about ten times per minute. Call an ambulance as soon as possible

(*c*) Clear all obstacles to prevent further injury. Do not attempt to force anything between the teeth as this could cause more damage than the patient biting his tongue. Afterwards, loosen tight clothing and cover the patient until he recovers.

21 (*a*) Smother the flames using a blanket or a heavy coat, or roll the waiter on the floor

(*b*) Lay the waiter on the floor and treat him for shock by loosening tight clothing. Cover his burns with a clean dry dressing. Cover him with a blanket to keep warm. Call the ambulance

(*c*) No attempt should be made to remove burnt clothing sticking to the skin, as this is sterile and more damage may be caused

(*d*) The waiter should not be given anything to eat or drink in case hospital treatment is needed.

Long-answer Questions

22 (*a*) *Deportment*

You are on your feet all day — it is important to stand up straight to prevent strain and backache

(*b*) *Clothing*

(i) *Shoes* — should be well fitting and comfortable giving an aid to good deportment

(ii) *Uniform* — should be clean, well pressed and changed regularly

(*c*) *Hair* — whatever the style, it should be washed and trimmed regularly

(*d*) *Skin*

(i) *Female*

- cleanse, tone and moisturise according to your skin type to prevent spots and dry patches
- do not use make-up and perfume to excess

(ii) *Male*

- wash face regularly and treat spots
- keep well shaven or trim beards and moustaches neatly
- do not use strong smelling after-shave or cologne

(*e*) *Nails*

Keep clean and well-shaped. Female receptionists should use nail polish sensibly

(*f*) *Teeth*

Clean and visit the dentist regularly. Bad teeth can cause bad breath

(*g*) *Personal Cleanliness*

Bath or shower daily. Do not use strong-smelling deodorants

(*h*) *Smoking*

Do not smoke in the reception area

(*i*) *Eating*

Do not eat food, sweets or chewing gum in the reception area

(*j*) *Speech*

Speak clearly in a pleasant tone.

23 (*a*) Let the guest have his say without interruption so that he can get the complaint 'off his chest'

(*b*) Pay attention to the details of his complaint and, if necessary, write them down. This helps you to ensure all points are covered, and also shows the guest you are taking the matter seriously

(*c*) Apologise on the hotel's behalf, without passing the blame on to any particular member of staff. Do *not* blame the guest

(*d*) Keep calm. Do not raise your voice and make the situation worse

(*e*) Recap each point and explain what action will be taken

(*f*) Complaints which require action beyond the receptionist's authority should be referred to management. If no one is available, explain that further action will be taken upon the manager's return

(*g*) Do not make promises which are beyond your authority or control.

24 *Introduction*

Before the receptionist can begin to sell the hotel's facilities, they must know what the hotel has to offer in the way of:

(*a*) rooms and the facilities within each room

(*b*) general facilities, e.g. lounges, swimming pool, saunas, sports facilities, meeting rooms

(*c*) food and beverage facilities, e.g. restaurants, bars, times of opening, menus

(*d*) prices/tariffs — special package rates etc.

Methods

(*a*) Quick assessment of customer's needs

(*b*) Creating needs for the customer

(*c*) Selling needs by pointing out the advantages and using lots of adjectives. For example, if a guest asks how much a room is, the receptionist should not just say 'It's *x* pounds'. She should add that this includes service charge and VAT and mention that the room has a private bathroom and very fine views over the Castle Gardens, if this is the case.

(NB. Be careful not to 'oversell', or the customer may be discouraged.)

(*d*) Offering an alternative to suit the customer's budget.

(*e*) Looking for additional sales opportunities in ordinary reservation letters. For example, a guest may mention that he is attending an international conference; contacting the conference organiser may bring the hotel more business.

(*f*) On departure, effort should be made to secure repeat business for your hotel or for another hotel within the group.

In addition to these, the receptionist will be supported by the sales department, e.g. brochures, mail shots and perhaps, Roomwatch and the local Tourist Board. Therefore, close co-operation is needed to give the customer up to the minute information and thus maximise sales.

25

1 T	R	A	V	2 E	L	■	3 B	4 A	T	5 H
A	■	■	■	N	■	6 P	■	M	■	O
7 C	O	U	R	T	E	S	Y	■	8 F	T
T	■	■	■	H	■	Y	■	9 M	■	E
■	10 B	■	11 P	U	N	C	T	U	A	L
12 S	A	L	■	S	■	H	■	M	■	S
13 P	G	■	14 C	I	R	O	C	■	15 Z	■
E	■	16 A	■	A	■	L	■	■	■	17 R
18 E	G	G	■	19 S	T	O	P	■	20 G	O
C	■	I	■	M	■	G	■	■	■	O
21 H	O	O	D	■	22 S	Y	S	T	E	M

PART THREE: ADVANCE RESERVATIONS

Multiple-choice Questions

1 a	2 c	3 b	4 a
5 b	6 a	7 a	8 d
9 d	10 d	11 d	12 b
13 a	14 b	15 c	16 c
17 c	18 c	19 a	20 a
21 c	22 b	23 d	24 c
25 b			

Short-answer Questions

26 (*a*) (i) Move Brown to 102, put reservation in 108

(ii) Move Hyde to 105, put Pearson in 103, put reservation in 104

(iii) Move reservation in 108 to 107, put McWilliams in 108, put reservation in 107

(*b*) (i) Reservation entries often have to be moved several times on the chart before the guest arrives in order to gain full occupancy

(ii) Short lengths of stay mean that entries have to be cramped and may become indecipherable

(iii) If the allocated room is not available when the guest arrives yet another alteration will have to be made.

27 (*a*) A hotel guest may be quoted a time to arrive by when he books. If he does not arrive by this time, his room will be available for reletting to another customer

(*b*) An office which takes reservations for a group of hotels which may belong to one company or a marketing consortium, e.g. Best Western

(*c*) A machine that transmits and receives written messages, through telephone lines, 24 hours a day, throughout the world

(*d*) A nationwide service by British Telecom in which telephones link television sets to a computer centre, enabling the user to receive thousands of 'pages' of data which includes information on hotels and room availability as well as other business information

(*e*) A room let for the daytime often for business meetings, or at an airport hotel, for air passengers and crew.

28 (*a*) The International Hotel Telegraph Code enables travellers to reserve accommodation avoiding language difficulties and reducing costs.

(*b*) (i) Arriving Wednesday morning, staying several days, meet at airport, one room with one bed and private bathroom of very good quality

(ii) One room with two beds and and child's bed, simple quality. Box for one motorcar. Staying one night. Arriving Sunday evening

(iii) RAWOW STOP ALDUA BELVU TRAIN 1500 hours

(iv) ANUL RAZEM RANUV PASS ABEC BON.

Long-answer Questions

29 *Introduction* – in-hotel systems, interhotel systems, future developments.

In-hotel systems

A comprehensive system should include the following facilities:

(*a*) reservations up to 18 months in advance:
  (i) individual
  (ii) group

(*b*) alternatives offered if preferred room not available

(*c*) pre-allocation of rooms if desired

(*d*) confirmation letter production by word processor software

(*e*) record of deposits paid

(*f*) cancellation or amendment of reservations

(*g*) reservation forecast production

(*h*) alphabetical list of expected arrivals for next day

(*i*) guest history file scanning procedure for marketing purposes

(*j*) alphabetical list of all reservations.

Interhotel systems — e.g. Holiday Inns' Holidex system.

Facilities include:

(*a*) reservations for all hotels within group

(*b*) alternative accommodation if selected room and/or hotel unavailable.

(*c*) linking reservations received with planned purchasing requirements and costing.

Future developments

(*a*) linking existing individual computers for worldwide coverage

(*b*) Prestel in UK — using television and telephone.

30 The following sections should be included in a well designed form:

(*a*) name of guest(s)

(*b*) home address and/or company name and address

(*c*) telephone number

(*d*) type of accommodation required — single, double etc.

(*e*) date of arrival and time of day

(*f*) length of stay

(*g*) special requirements; sea view

(*h*) date of booking

(*i*) tariff

(*j*) (entered in) diary

(*k*) (entered on) chart

(*l*) deposit paid

(*m*) receptionist's signature

(*n*) source of reservation

(*o*) release time (if applicable)

(*p*) confirmation required

(*q*) cancellation

(*r*) amendment.

This is how it may be laid out:

Name . CRACKER J.B.	Arrival date . . 1-6-82
Surname Initials ~~Mr~~/Mrs/~~Miss~~	AM (PM)
Address . . 222 WESTBOURNE EST.	No. of nights 2
WESTHAMPTON	Depart. date . . 3-6-82
HERTS	(Hold)/Release
WS4 6JP	Type of accommodation:
Telephone . . 025-617-9210	S _ SB 1 D _ DB _ T _ TB _
Company name . CRACKER BISCUITS LTD.,	Charted . . . RS.
Company contact . MISS WILLIAMS X 211	Date booked . . 6-4-82
Account instructions . A/C TO CRACKER	Rate £ . 32-50
BISCUITS LTD. AT ABOVE ADDRESS	How booked:
Special requirements/remarks . . . V.I.P.	Self ☑
	Group ☐
	Agent ☐
TBC ☑ NTBC ☐	C.R.O. ☐
By guest ☑ By hotel ☐	Other ☐
Confirmed on . . 8-4-82	
Cancelled on	Amended on . . . . . .
Deposit paid £	Booking taken by . . RS.

31 Your answer should describe the following sequence of events:

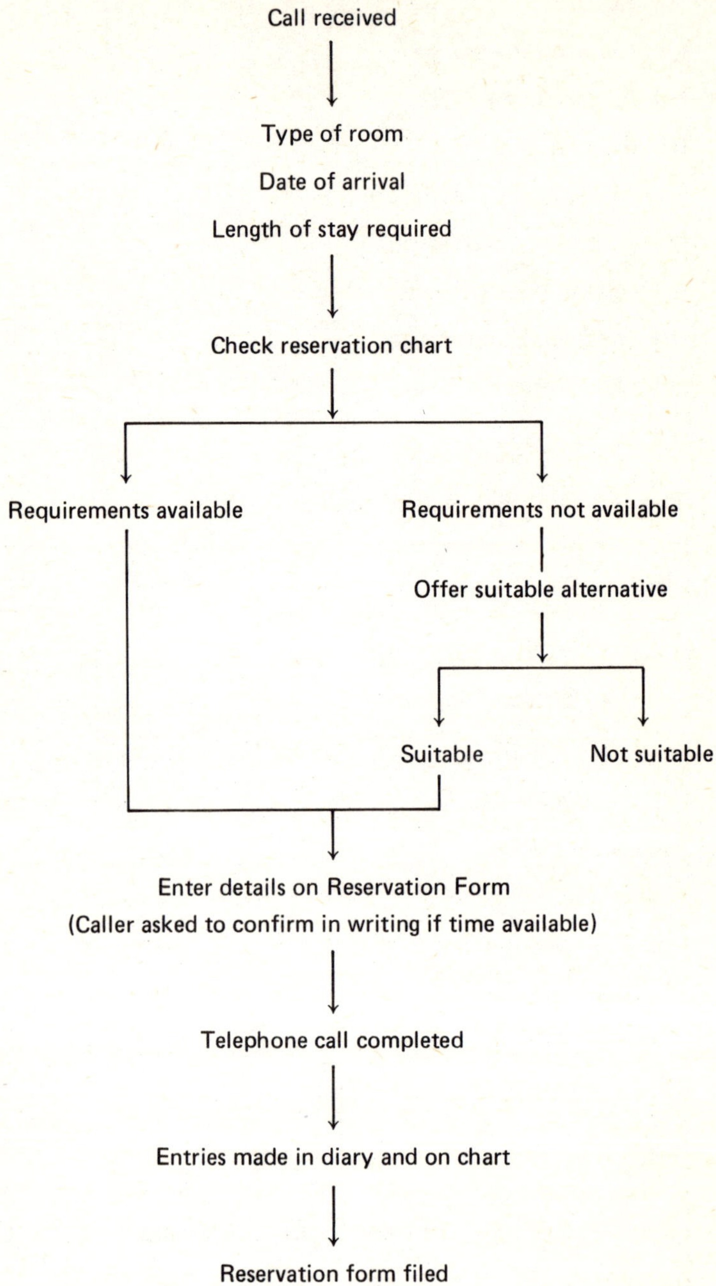

32 (*a*) *Density chart*

JUNE 19 __

	1	2	3	4	5	6	7	8	9	10	11	12	13	14
SB 5	/	/	/	/	/	/	/	/	/	/	/	/	/	
4		/	/	/	/	/	/			/	/	/	/	
3		/	/	/	/									
2			/	/										
1				/										
DB 10	/	/	/	/	/	/	/	/	/	/	/			
9	/	/	/	/	/	/	/	/	/	/				
8				/	/	/	/							
7				/	/									
6				/	/									
5				/	/									
4				/	/									
3				/	/									
2					/									
1														
TB 6	/	/	/	/										
5	/	/												
4														
3														
2														
1														

(*b*) *Hotel reservations diary*

Day: TUESDAY			Date: JUNE 2nd	
Name	Type of room	Terms	Length of stay	Remarks
~~FORD MR.~~	~~DB.~~	~~AO.~~	~~5N~~	~~Cancelled 6/5 GB.~~
OXFORD MR.	2 SB	RB	3N	1 x Garage.

Day: WEDNESDAY			Date: JUNE 3rd	
Name	Type of room	Terms	Length of stay	Remarks
~~SANDMAN MR.~~	~~SB~~	~~AO.~~	~~2N.~~	~~Cancelled 12/4 GB.~~
BROWN MRS.	SB	INC.	11 N.	£50 deposit.

PART FOUR: RECEPTION PROCEDURES

Multiple-choice Questions

1 b	2 d	3 d	4 d
5 a	6 b	7 c	8 a
9 d	10 d	11 b	12 a
13 c	14 d	15 d	16 b
17 c	18 c	19 a	20 c
21 c	22 a	23 b	24 c
25 b	26 b	27 c	28 a
29 c	30 b	31 b	32 a
33 b	34 c	35 d	36 b

Short-answer Questions

37 (*a*) (i) Say 'name of hotel, good morning/afternoon/evening, Reception can I help you?'

(ii) 'Reception, can I help you?'

(*b*) Say, 'Excuse me whilst I answer the telephone'
Deal with the telephone call as efficiently as possible. Return to the guest at reception, apologising for the interruption.

38 You should politely tell her that, as you have not received any instructions from Mr Banks himself, you cannot allow her into his room. You should then suggest that she takes a seat in the hotel lounge and perhaps orders a drink until he arrives. A note should be left with Mr Banks' key so that he can be informed of his sister's arrival.

Long-answer Questions

39

To be completed by all guests Please print	
Surname	Christian Names
Full home address	Nationality
	Car Reg. No.
Company name and address	
Please indicate how you intend to settle your account (tick)	Cash . . . Company . . . Credit card . . . Other . . .
Credit card name	Card number
(For overseas visitors only) Passport number Place of issue Next destination	I will depart on . . . . Signature Date
For office use Room No.	Rate £ No. in party

The Immigration (Hotel Records) Order 1972 requires that all guests aged 16 and over must supply their full name, date of arrival and nationality.

The Aliens Orders of 1953 and 1957 require that all guests who are not British or Commonwealth citizens must provide the following information: passport number and its place of issue, their date of departure, and next destination including the address if known. Exceptions to this are persons covered by the Diplomatic Privileges Act 1964, i.e. Ambassadors and their families and staff who need not register at all, and also persons serving with the British or NATO armed forces who can register as if they were British subjects.

40 *Brief description of electronic key systems available*

A computer console in Reception issues key cards which are programmed at random with any one of several billion code numbers.

By inserting the key card into the door lock, which is usually completely independent of the computer, the door lock is programmed to accept that particular combination until another new key card is used.

Each lock has its own series of combinations so that each key card can only open one door.

Advantages

(*a*) *Security.*

- (i) Every new guest receives a completely new key with a new combination. Therefore previous guests cannot re-enter the room.
- (ii) Guests sharing rooms can receive identical keys
- (iii) Lost keys can be replaced with entirely new keys with new combinations
- (iv) Sub master, master and grand master keys are available, and if lost or stolen, sections or the whole hotel can be reprogrammed for new masters

(*b*) It saves the expense of changing traditional locks and using duplicate keys should a key be lost, stolen or taken away by a departing guest in error.

Disadvantages

(*a*) Initial capital cost

(*b*) Cost of blank key cards.

41 (*a*) Room occupancy $= \dfrac{\text{Number of rooms sold}}{\text{Number of rooms available}} \times \dfrac{100}{1}$

Monday: $\frac{29}{50} \times \frac{100}{1} =$ 58%

Tuesday: 60%

Wednesday: 96%

Thursday: 100%

Friday: 66%

Saturday: 48%

Sunday: 20%

Week: $\frac{224}{350} \times \frac{100}{1} =$ 64%

(*b*) Sleeper occupancy $= \frac{\text{Number of sleepers}}{\text{Total sleeper capacity}} \times \frac{100}{1}$

Monday: $\frac{52}{90} \times \frac{100}{1} =$ 58%

Tuesday: 61%

Wednesday: 98%

Thursday: 100%

Friday: 60%

Saturday: 47%

Sunday: 19%

Week: $\frac{398}{630} \times \frac{100}{1} =$ 63%

(*c*) Double occupancy $= \frac{\text{No of doubles/twins let as doubles}}{\text{No of doubles/twins available}} \times \frac{100}{1}$

Monday: $\frac{23}{40} \times \frac{100}{1} =$ 58%

Tuesday: 63%

Wednesday: 100%

Thursday: 100%

Friday: 53%

Saturday: 45%

Sunday: 18%

Week: $\frac{174}{280} \times \frac{100}{1} =$ 62%

(*d*) Average room rate $= \dfrac{\text{Income}}{\text{Number of rooms sold}}$

Monday: $\dfrac{1030}{29} = £35.52$

Tuesday: $\dfrac{1100}{30} = £36.67$

Wednesday: $\dfrac{1760}{48} = £36.67$

Thursday: $\dfrac{1800}{50} = £36.00$

Friday: $\dfrac{1100}{33} = £33.33$

Saturday: $\dfrac{850}{24} = £35.42$

Sunday: $\dfrac{354}{10} = £34.50$

Week: $\dfrac{7985}{224} = £35.66$

(*e*) Income occupancy $= \dfrac{\text{Income}}{\text{Total possible income}} \times \dfrac{100}{1}$

Monday: $\dfrac{1030}{1800} = 57\%$

Tuesday: 61%

Wednesday: 98%

Thursday: 100%

Friday: 61%

Saturday: 47%

Sunday: 19%

Week: $\dfrac{7985}{12600} = 63\%$

PART FIVE: CASHIERS

Multiple-choice Questions

1 c	2 b	3 d	4 b
5 d	6 b	7 c	8 a
9 d	10 d	11 c	12 b
13 d	14 d	15 a	16 b
17 b	18 c	19 a	20 b
21 b	22 a	23 d	24 d
25 d	26 b	27 a	28 b
29 d	30 b	31 c	32 a
33 b	34 a	35 b	36 d
37 a	38 d	39 d	40 a
41 b	42 c	43 a	44 b
45 d			

Short-answer Questions

46

Petty Cash Voucher	Date 27/9/80
Details	Amount
Chef's Taxi Fare	£2.50
Total	£ 2.50
Received by: A. Chef.	Authorised by: A. Supervisor.

47 *Definition:* A sum of money of small denominations for the purpose of giving change and exchanging foreign currency.

Determinants of float size:

(*a*) prices charged

(*b*) number of payments

(*c*) methods of payment

NB. Also consider security and that floats use money that could be invested.

48 *Definition:* An accurate method of giving change, building from the amount payable up to the amount tendered.

Example:	Amount payable	£2.67
	Amount tendered	£5.00

Build and say aloud to the customer, counting the change into his hand:

	'£2.67'
+ 1p	'£2.68'
+ 2p	'£2.70'
+ 10p	'£2.80'
+ 10p	'£2.90'
+ 10p	'£3.00'
+ £1	'£4.00'
+ £1	'£5.00'

49 Clearance of a cheque

Guest gives cheque to cashier

↓

Cashier deposits cheque in hotel's bank
Hotel's account credited – but cheque uncleared

(→ If the guest and the hotel use the same bank group, a cheque is cleared directly through the computer system → Guest's account debited)

↓

Cheque goes to head office of hotel's bank

↓

Cheque goes to clearing house

↓

Cheque goes to head office of guest's bank

↓

Cheque goes to branch of guest's bank
Guest's account debited

50

	Bank cheque card		*Credit card*
(*a*)	Must be presented with a cheque	(*a*)	Presented alone and card details imprinted onto voucher
(*b*)	Guarantees payment of cheque up to £50.00	(*b*)	Allows purchase of goods and services up to a predetermined credit limit
(*c*)	Hotels can accept cheques and cheque cards from all banks	(*c*)	Hotels can only accept credit cards from those credit card companies with which they have an arrangement.

Long-answer Questions

51 *Ledger accounts*

Introduction: Definition of ledger accounts

(*a*) individual accounts

(*b*) business accounts

Advantages:

(*a*) encourages customer loyalty

(*b*) encourages greater expenditure

(*c*) encourages repeat business

Disadvantages:

(*a*) delay in receipt of payment

(*b*) risk of bad debts

(*c*) extra administration costs

Conclusion: Summary and decision on value to hotel of ledger accounts.

52

	PETTY CASH BOOK								
Receipts	Date	Details	V. No.	Total	Post	Prov	Trav.	Stat.	VPO
20.00	Aug 1	Bal. b/d							
	Aug 1	Postage stamps	32	6.50	6.50				
	Aug 2	Blackledge R.127 Dry cleaning	33	2.25					2.25
	Aug 3	Waitresses' fares	34	1.50			1.50		
	Aug 4	Whitlock R.316 Taxi	35	5.30					5.30
	Aug 4	Bapat the Baker Bread	36	2.00		2.00			
	Aug 5	Typing paper	37	0.75				0.75	
	Aug 7	Davey R.321 COD parcel	38	0.90					0.90
				19.20	6.50	2.00	1.50	0.75	8.45
		Bal. c/d		0.80					
20.00				20.00					
0.80	Aug 8	Bal. b/d							
19.20	Aug 8	Cash							

53 *Bank Cheque Card*

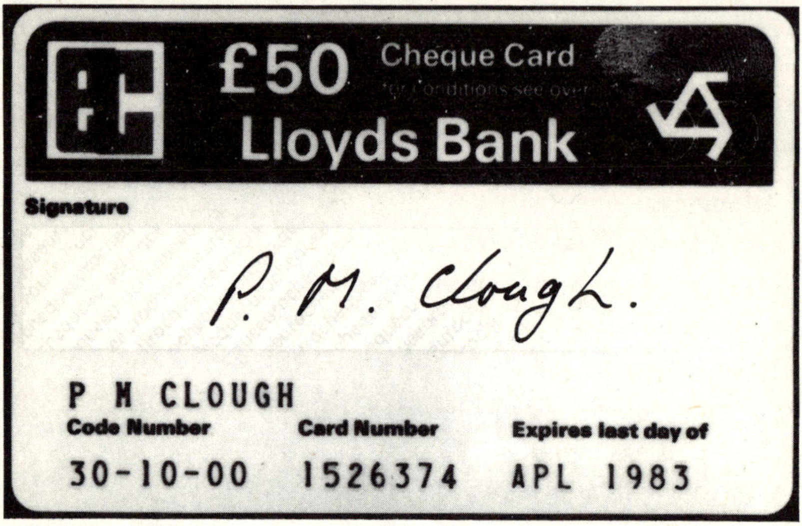

Points to verify

(*a*) The cheque must be signed in the presence of the cashier

(*b*) The date on cheque must be correct

(*c*) The words and figures must agree

(*d*) The code number on the card must be the same as the bank code number on the top right-hand corner of the cheque

(*e*) The name of the payee must be correct

(*f*) Any alterations must be counter-signed

(*g*) The signature on the cheque must be the same as that on the cheque card

(*h*) If all these are satisfactory, write the cheque card number on the reverse of the cheque.

54 *Banking procedure*

(*a*) Sort cash into various denominations and currencies

(*b*) Bag coins:
$\frac{1}{2}$p in 50p bags
1p in 50p bags
2p in 50p bags
5p in £5 bags
10p in £5 bags
50p in £10 bags

(*c*) Face notes:
£1 notes in £100 bands
£5 notes in £500 bands
£10 notes in £500 bands
£20 notes in £1000 bands
£50 notes in £500 bands

(*d*) List each cheque on the reverse of the paying-in slip – detail the name of the drawer, the bank sorting code, and the amount

(*e*) Enter details on the front of the paying-in slip: coins, notes, total of cheques, date, who paid in by

(*f*) Complete a separate paying-in slip for foreign currencies

(*g*) Complete a separate paying-in slip for bank-affiliated credit cards.

NB. A duplicate or triplicate paying-in book is often used to provide the hotel and head office with a copy of each day's banking details.

PART SIX: BOOK KEEPING

Multiple-choice Questions

1 d	2 a	3 c	4 d
5 b	6 d	7 c	8 d
9 b	10 b	11 a	12 c
13 a	14 b	15 d	16 c

Short-answer Questions

17

OPUS OPERATIC SOCIETY A/C

14/4	Bal b/f	256.67	14/4	By cash	96.42
14/4	To Luncheon	87.59			
			14/4	Bal c/d	247.84
		344.26			344.26
14/4	Bal b/d	247.84			

CASH BOOK

		Cash	Bank			Cash	Bank
14/4	To Opus Operatic	96.42					

18 A cash discount may be given to encourage prompt settlement of a bill. It is shown in the supplier's account in the purchases ledger as discount received.

A trade discount may be given to the hotel because it buys in large quantities. This is not usually shown in the purchases ledger, but the net amount that the hotel owes is. Further cash discounts for prompt payment may be given on this amount as well.

19 The amount should be entered in Room 17's column on today's tabular ledger under 'Wine', and yesterday's date should be written above the amount and circled. Mr Quick's bill should also be adjusted in the same way. The wine waiter's check should be endorsed by writing 'posted on (today's date)'. This is called *back-dating*.

20 The tabular ledger sheet is split into two parts: Debit and Credit, as illustrated by this example from a vertical ledger.

Apartments	
Pension	
Breakfast	
Luncheon	
Teas	
Dinners	
Early teas	
Beverages	
Wines	
Spirits/Liqueurs	
Beers	DEBIT
Minerals	
Telephones	
U.P.O.'s	
Tobacco	
Newspapers	
Daily Total	
Balance b/fwd	
Grand total	

(*continued overleaf*)

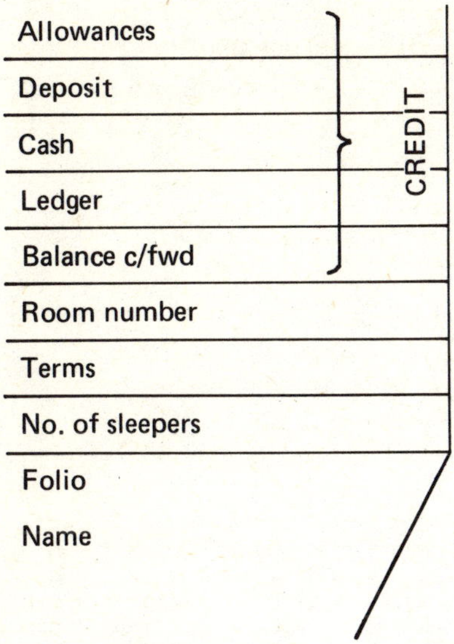

(*a*) Visitors' charges are debited to their individual accounts in the tabular ledger and thus transferred to the daily and then monthly summary. The monthly summary totals are then credited to the appropriate sales accounts, e.g. for telephones

(*b*) Cash received from visitors is credited to their individual accounts in the tabular ledger, with the corresponding debits in the cash book

(*c*) VPOs are debited to the visitors' individual tabular ledger accounts and are credited to the petty cash book

(*d*) Allowances are credited to the visitors' accounts and thus transferred to the monthly allowance sheet with the corresponding debit in the appropriate sales account, e.g. for Wines.

21 (*a*) The shift key is used to identify morning or afternoon shifts or individual operators

(*b*) The X key lists the totals of the debit and credit keys to show the business done so far and, to balance the machine

(*c*) The Z key lists the totals of the debit and credit keys and also clears the machine.

22 Selling price $= \dfrac{\text{Food cost}}{\text{Food cost \%}} \times 100$ (Food cost % = 100% – Gross profit %)

(*a*) £0.625

(*b*) £1.30

(*c*) £3.79

(*d*) £3.06

(*e*) £1.38.

23 Gross profit % = $\frac{\text{Gross profit}}{\text{Selling price}} \times 100$ (Gross profit = Selling price – Food cost)

(*a*) 60%
(*b*) 67.5%
(*c*) 67.1%
(*d*) 53.8%
(*e*) 68.7%

Long-answer Questions

24 (*a*)

Employee	Net pay	£50.00	£20.00	£10.00	£5.00	£1.00	50p	10p	5p	2p	1p
Renton	46.98	–	40.00	–	5.00	1.00	0.50	0.40	0.05	0.02	0.01
Flood	116.43	100.00	–	10.00	5.00	1.00	–	0.40	–	0.02	0.01
Gamble	37.02	–	20.00	10.00	5.00	2.00	–	–	–	0.02	–
Bird	78.16	50.00	20.00	–	5.00	3.00	–	0.10	0.05	–	0.01
Robinson	12.68	–	–	10.00	–	2.00	0.50	0.10	0.05	0.02	0.01
Totals	291.27	150.00	80.00	30.00	20.00	9.00	1.00	1.00	0.15	0.08	0.04

(*b*) (i) The personal tax code gives the total of personal tax-free allowances

(ii) Tax table A shows weekly and monthly tax free pay to date for every tax code

(iii) Tax table B shows tax due to be paid on the taxable pay which has been calculated by using the figures in tax table A.

25 (*a*) (i) To prove it arithmetically correct

(ii) To analyse the business done during the day into departments. This information is then transferred onto the summary sheet.

(*b*) (i) errors of omission
errors of commission
compensating errors

(ii) Errors of omission can occur when:

(1) Charge vouchers are lost and no entry is made on the guest's account. These can only be detected by the control office

(2) The charge has been entered on the visitor's bill, but not on the tabular ledger. This will be revealed when the balances on the tab. are compared against the balances on the guests' bills at the end of each day

(3) A guest's account brought forward figure is omitted. To prevent this, the brought forward figures should be carried forward from the previous day's ledger and totalled. This total should be the same as the balance *carried* forward on the tabular ledger for the previous day.

(iii) Errors of commission can occur when:

(1) The wrong amount is posted to a guest's account

(2) The correct amount is posted to the wrong guest's account

(3) The correct amount is posted to the wrong analysis column, e.g. Dinners to Luncheons.

These errors may be detected by guests querying their bills or by the control office.

(iv) Compensating errors can occur when an arithmetical error is cancelled out by one or more others. Comparing individual guest's bills with the tabular ledger at the end of each day will indicate these.

26 (*a*) An allowance has to be made to room 23 by entering £15.86 in room 23's allowances column on the tabular ledger and also recording this entry in the Allowances Book stating the nature of the error. The bill for room 23 should be corrected by ruling through the incorrect posting and entering the same amount in the allowances column. The charge of £15.86 should then be entered in the dinner column under room 33 on the tabular ledger and back dated by writing yesterday's date in a circle above. £15.86 should then be posted under dinner on room 33's bill

(*b*) See the diagram on p. 76

(*c*) The Allowances Book is used by management for control purposes and also to adjust the summary sheet, e.g. there would now be two postings of £15.86 for dinner.

Month: December

ALLOWANCES BOOK

Date	Reason	Authorised by	Apartments	Pension	Breakfast	Luncheons	Teas	Dinners	Early Teas	Beverages	Wines	Spirits	Beers	Minerals	Telephones	Tobacco	Total
12·12·81	Charge posted in error to Room 23 instead of 33.	A. Manager.						15·86									15·86
Totals																	

27 *Advantages:*

(*a*) It is faster and more accurate than a manual system

(*b*) Records are neat and legible

(*c*) One has an individual hotel program and keyboard layout, giving wide range of analysis and management information

(*d*) Other special features include:

- (i) charge transfer from point of sale, i.e. terminal in hotel bar automatically adds charges to guest's account
- (ii) automatic balance pick-up
- (iii) automatic posting of correct room rate
- (iv) compulsory sequence control ensuring correct procedure is followed
- (v) currency conversion
- (vi) automatic tax and service charge calculations
- (vii) cashiers' shift report, analysing methods of payment for cash control
- (viii) revenue report, giving a complete analysis of all charges

(*e*) Ability to link satellite units to main machine.

Factors to be considered when purchasing such a machine:

(*a*) availability of money

(*b*) business turnover

(*c*) detail of analysis required

(*d*) safeguards against fraud

(*e*) ease of operation, staff training, and staff turnover

(*f*) after-sales service, breakdown maintenance, service contracts, reprogramming facilities

(*g*) cost of specialised stationery

(*h*) size; space available

(*i*) technical specifications.

28

Apartments		12·00	20·00		24·0
Pension					
Breakfast		2·00	2·00		4·0
Luncheons		4·00	4·00		8·0
Teas					
Dinners			(12/12/81) 2·00		
Early teas	0·80	0·40	0·40	0·40	0·8
Beverages		0·60 0·40	0·60		1·2 0·8
Wines			2·24		
Spirits/Liqueurs					3·0
Beers		0·56			
Minerals					
Telephones	1·20	1·80	0·80	0·80	2·2
VPOs		6·00			
Tobacco					1·0
Newspapers	1·20	0·40		0·20	
Daily total	3·20	28·16	32·04	1·40	45·0
Balance b/fwd	116·72	60·44	14·00	28·00	49·4
Grand total	119·92	88·60	46·04	29·40	94·4
Allowances					0·8
Deposit	20·00				
Cash	99·92			29·40	40·0
Ledger					
Balance c/fwd		88·60	46·04		53·6
Room number	14 DB	31 ~~20~~ S ~~SB~~	25 SB	31 S	32 T
Terms	INC.	R + B.	R + B.	INC.	R + B
No of sleepers	2	1	1	1	2
Folio					
Name	MR/S B. WEST	MR. P. PARKER	MISS R. ROSE	MR. R. ASHMORE	MR/S. J. WEBB

2.00					22.00		110.00
24.00							24.00
						34.00	42.00
					440.00	100.80	556.80
							2.00
							2.80
0.80						7.00 8.40	19.80
					96.00	19.80	118.04
				199.30	60.00	27.20	289.50
				21.60			22.16
0.60						0.44	1.04
						9.80	16.60
							6.00
					30.00	4.56	35.56
							1.80
7.40				220.90	648.00	212.00	1248.10
-					-	-	268.60
7.40				220.90	648.00	212.00	1516.70
							0.80
							20.00
				220.90		212.00	602.22
					648.00		648.00
7.40							245.68
4 DB							
INC.							
2							6
AWLEY				LOUNGE BAR	R/1 ROTARY CLUB	CHANCE	

29

Apartments	65.00		60.00	65.0
Pension				36.0
Breakfast	10.00 10.00		10.00	
Luncheons	15.10		15.10	
Teas	2.50		2.50	
Dinners	20.60		20.60	
Early teas	1.00	1.00	1.00	1.0
Beverages	1.30 1.00		1.30 1.00	1.30 1.00
Wines	6.36			4.25
Spirits/Liqueurs				
Beers				0.70
Minerals				
Telephones			0.75	
VPOs				6.5
Tobacco				1.25
Newspapers				
Refund		36.71		
Daily total	132.86	37.71	112.25	117.0
Balance b/fwd	201.63	62.29	(16.92)	36.3
Grand total	334.49	100.00	95.33	153.4
Allowances				10.0
Deposit		100.00		
Cash				
Ledger				
Balance c/fwd	334.49		95.33	143.4
Room number	101 DB	209 TB	210 T	304
Terms	E.P.	C.P.	C.P.	A.P.
No of sleepers	2	2	2	2
Folio				
Name	MR/S BALDWIN	MAJOR Y MRS. PHILPOTT	MR/S CAPLAND	MR/S COWLEY

5.00	30.00	65.00	35.00			5.00		360.00
		36.00						72.00
5.00	5.00							40.00
	7.55					410.55	271.80	720.16
1.25	1.25		1.25				45.00	53.75
10.30	10.30		10.30					72.10
0.50	0.50							5.00
0.65	0.65 0.50	1.00	0.50				3.25	13.45
	9.88	16.01				25.00	16.52 52.51	130.53
	1.67				25.95			27.62
					16.52			17.22
	0.62							1.37
								6.56
					12.76		5.93	19.94
								36.71
52.70	67.92	118.01	47.05		55.23	440.55	395.01	1576.35
49.61	111.01	–	–		–	–	–	444.01
02.31	178.93	118.01	47.05		55.23	440.55	395.01	2020.36
								10.00
								100.00
50.00		505.00			55.23		392.51	1102.74
						440.55	AMEX 2.50	443.05
47.69)	178.93	(386.99)	47.05					364.57
05 SB	309 S	209 TB	102 SB					
C.P.	E.P.	A.P.	E.P.					
1	1	2	1					11
WHITE	MR. CRABTREE	MR/S JACKSON	MR. GRAHAM.		COCKTAIL BAR.	P/165 PICKARD SCHOOL OF MOTORING	CHANCE	

30

Apartments		45.00	46.00	45.00	
Pension		30.00		30.00	
Breakfast			5.00		
Luncheons			11.50		(12/12) 5.7
Teas					
Dinners					
Early teas	1.00	1.00	1.00	1.00	0.5
Beverages		1.20 0.55	1.20 1.10	1.20	
Wines	(12/12) 6.50		5.92		
Spirits/Liqueurs		0.90			
Beers					
Minerals					
Telephones	0.16			0.32	
VPOs					
Tobacco					
Newspapers		0.15		0.25	0.3
Daily total	7.66	78.80	71.72	77.77	6.5
Balance b/fwd	193.07	64.72	(20.27)	53.48	42.71
Grand total	200.73	143.52	51.45	131.25	49.2
Allowances					
Deposit	100.00				
Cash	100.73		75.00		49.26
Ledger					
Balance c/fwd		143.52	(23.55)	131.25	
Room number	201 DB	309 TB	310 T	404 DB	405 S
Terms	R+B	INC.	R+B	INC.	R+B
No of sleepers	2	2	2	2	1
Folio					
Name	MR/S GUTTERIDGE	CAPT. + MRS. STEVENS	MR/S BRIGGS	MR/S WILLIAMS	MISS BAPAT

	MR. SWEETLAND	WHISTLE STOP TOURS. W/1			ALPHA AERO CLUB A/2	CHANCE	
·00	20·00	280·00			5·00		466·00
·00	15·00						90·00
		40·00				12·50	57·50
·75					139·00	69·00	231·00
·50							5·00
·60					11·00	9·60 5·50	31·95
0·39						20·51 15·72	59·04
1·20							2·10
					25·00		25·00
							–
·25							1·73
							–
·50							2·50
							0·70
·19	35·00	320·00			180·00	132·83	972·52
·50	–	–			–	–	448·21
·69	35·00	320·00			180·00	132·83	1420·73
5·75							5·75
							100·00
	245·00					132·83	602·82
		320·00			180·00		500·00
·94	(210·00)						212·16
5 53 9 S	409 S	501-508 D			MASON SUITE		
NC	INC	R+B					
1	1	16					24

Bibliography

Accommodation Operations by Colin Dix (published by Macdonald and Evans)

A Manual of Hotel Reception by J R S Beavis and S Medlik (published by Heinemann)

Hotel Reception by Paul B White and Helen Beckley (published by Edward Arnold)

Hotel Information Systems by Michael L Kasavana (published by CBI Publishing Company Inc)

Hotel and Catering Law by David Field (published by Sweet and Maxwell)